FROM RUTH'S KITCHEN WITH LOVE

FROM RUTH'S KITCHEN
WITH LOVE

DELICIOUS BUKOVINIAN & OTHER ETHNIC DISHES

Ruth Glasberg Gold

iUniverse, Inc.
Bloomington

FROM RUTH'S KITCHEN WITH LOVE
DELICIOUS BUKOVINIAN & OTHER ETHNIC DISHES

iUniverse books may be ordered through booksellers or by contacting:

iUniverse
1663 Liberty Drive
Bloomington, IN 47403
www.iuniverse.com
1-800-Authors (1-800-288-4677)

Because of the dynamic nature of the Internet, any web addresses or links contained in this book may have changed since publication and may no longer be valid. The views expressed in this work are solely those of the author and do not necessarily reflect the views of the publisher, and the publisher hereby disclaims any responsibility for them.

ISBN: 978-1-4502-5238-6 (pbk)
ISBN: 978-1-4502-5240-9 (ebk)

Printed in the United States of America

iUniverse rev. date: 03/14/2011

DEDICATION

This book is first and foremost dedicated to my precious and multi-talented granddaughter Ariel, in the hope that she will recreate the traditional dishes from the recipes in this book and pass them on to future generations.

I am also dedicating it to my grandson Alexander, my daughter Liana, my son Michael and my daughter-in-law Fanny, with love.

ACKNOWLEDGMENTS

My special debt of gratitude goes to all my relatives and friends who shared their recipes with me, thus contributing to the creation of this cookbook. You are all a part of this project. I owe special thanks to Marisol Solis Marroquin (Monterrey, Mexico) for her invaluable help in the production of the cover.

INTRODUCTION

In northeastern Romania, at the folds of the Carpathian Mountains with its rolling hills, towering mountains, and dense ancient forests of beech trees, lies a province of breathtaking beauty, called Bukovina. In Romanian, in literary or poetic contexts, the name is Țara Fagilor (the land of beech trees). This province was truly my native land, and Czernowitz, its capital, my hometown.

Over the centuries many nations and empires fought for and conquered this region: the Tatars, the Greeks, the Ottoman Turks, the Austro-Hungarian Empire, and the Soviet Union. Today Bukovina is split between Romania and Ukraine.

Until 1940, Bukovina was a province blessed with extraordinary cultural, social, and ethnic diversity; its cuisine was an international mélange of dishes from different cultures.

This region was home to many ethnic groups: Ruthenians (Ukrainians), Romanians, Romas (Gypsies), Hutzulians (Ukrainian Highlanders), Poles, Germans, and Jews. We all coexisted peacefully until 1940 when the Soviets occupied North Bukovina and the subsequent outbreak of WWII. Then everything changed.

It was a world that is no longer.

As a result of that terrible war, I was orphaned and would not have a home again until 1958, when I married my husband, Salomon Gold, and settled in Bogotá Colombia. Prior to that, I never had the opportunity to learn to cook or bake. My expertise was limited to making fried eggs, sunny side up. Challenging myself was nothing new, so I ventured into this new undertaking, equipped with only a strong willpower and ambition. I started with a single Viennese cookbook and recipes sent to me by my aunts and other relatives. It was by trial and error and many culinary disasters that I eventually managed to put together a decent meal for my husband and me. The birth of my son and then my daughter increased my motivation and enthusiasm.

As Marcel Proust said: "The smell and taste of things remain poised a long time." That was very true in my case. From pure memory, I reconstructed the tastes of dishes my mother used to prepare, and that helped me a lot. Within a few years, my cooking and baking improved so much that I was able to entertain my friends with sit-down dinners and large parties. To my great amazement, they enjoyed my dishes and sincerely praised my culinary talent. Ironically, I was soon labeled as a "great cook."

Although my happy childhood ended when I was only eleven, some memories remain deeply engraved, particularly those tastes and smells of my mother's and my aunts' delicacies. I want to preserve this heritage with this unpretentious cookbook.

I included mostly traditional recipes from the Bukovina and its vicinity, as well as some Eastern European Jewish recipes, but I also included my own repertoire of dishes that I adopted from the various countries I visited or lived in, such as Romania, Russia, Ukraine, Austria, Israel, and Colombia.

It is my special pleasure to mention that, for the past fifty years, all the recipes in this book were prepared by me and served to my family and at my large dinner parties.

I hope to encourage others to engage in this creative hobby, as it is not only fun, but it is also a means of giving pleasure to others.

Bon appétit!

Table of Contents

APPETIZERS

CALF'S FOOT JELLY (Sueltze/Petcha)

Serves 8

2½	pounds calf's or pig's feet
10	cloves crushed garlic
1	medium onion, quartered
2	carrots, peeled and sliced
2	hard-boiled eggs
2	bay leaves
1	clove
1	tablespoon vinegar
1	tablespoon salt
½	teaspoon white pepper
1	teaspoon pickled capers
1	lemon sliced
7	pints cold water
2	teaspoons salt

Have the butcher cut the calf's feet in pieces and wash them thoroughly. Put the pieces in a saucepan, cover with water, bring to a boil at a high temperature, and boil rapidly for two to three minutes. Discard the water and cover the feet with fresh cold water.

Add the onions, bay leaf, carrots, and one tablespoon of salt. Partially cover the pot, bring to a boil, and cook over very low heat for about six hours, or until the meat separates from the bone. The broth should be reduced by half. Remove from the stove. Discard the onions and carrots. Lift the bones from the pot, remove the meat, and chop finely. Strain the liquid through several layers of cheesecloth into a clean bowl. Make sure the liquid is reduced to about three pints.

Mix the shredded meat with the crushed garlic, and salt and pepper to taste. Separately, slice the hard-boiled eggs. Line a rectangular Pyrex, or similar dish, with foil and brush it with some vegetable oil. Arrange the egg circles at the bottom, spread the meat mixture on top, and slowly pour the broth over the meat. Allow to cool and refrigerate covered overnight. The next day, remove any fat from the surface, run a knife around the edges, and place the Pyrex on top of a hot kitchen towel, soaked in hot water or warmed in a microwave, to loosen the mold. Cover with a serving platter and invert the jelly onto the plate. You may want to put some capers in the center of each egg slice and garnish with lemon slices. Serve with mustard or horseradish.

Cooking Tip:
The same recipe can be made with chicken feet, necks, and giblets.

CHOPPED CHICKEN LIVERS

Serves 12

1	pound chicken livers
3	tablespoons vegetable oil
1	large onion
½	teaspoon chicken instant bouillon
1	tomato
1	green bell pepper
	salt and pepper to taste

In a large skillet, fry the livers for about 15-20 minutes. Remove them from skillet and let them cool. Chop the onion and sauté it in the same oil until light brown. Chop the livers together with the sautéed onion. Dissolve the bouillon in one teaspoon hot water and add it to the livers. Taste for salt and pepper. Decorate with tomato and green bell pepper slices.

FASOLE BATUTA (Bean paste; a Romanian specialty)

Although this is a typical Romanian recipe, the Jews adopted it and ate it on Saturdays as a lunch appetizer.

Serves 8

1½	cups cannellini beans (canned)
3	tablespoons vegetable oil
1	medium onion, thinly sliced
3	cloves garlic, pressed
1	teaspoon sweet paprika
	salt and pepper to taste

Originally one would have to boil dried beans to prepare this dish, which takes a long time. I modified the recipe by using canned beans and was quite satisfied with the result.

Drain the beans, but reserve some of the liquid for later. In a large pan, fry the onions in very hot oil until light brown. Add the paprika and mix well with the onions. Remove from heat. With a slotted spoon remove the onions from the pan and let drain on a paper towel. Let the oil cool for a few minutes. Puree the beans in a food processor with some of their own liquid, and gradually add small amounts of the onion oil, like in mayonnaise. The paste should be creamy and foamy. Add the garlic, pepper, and salt. Arrange on a flat serving platter and garnish with the fried onions.

HERRING SALAD

Serves 6

3	matjes herring filets
1½	cups diced cooked beets
1½	cups diced cooked potatoes
3	apples (not peeled), diced
3	teaspoons capers
2	dill pickles, diced
½	cup chopped onions
½	teaspoon black pepper

For the dressing

1	cup sour cream
2	tablespoons red wine vinegar
1	teaspoon Dijon mustard
½	teaspoon salt
2	tablespoons sugar
1	cup chopped parsley

Cook the potatoes in their skin, peel, and dice. Cook the beets in a pressure cooker; cool, peel, and dice. (Canned beets may be used.) Cut the herring into small pieces. In a salad bowl, toss together all the ingredients.

Whisk together all the ingredients, pour over the salad, and toss it lightly. Cover and chill. Serve the salad garnished with parsley.

LIPTAUER CHEESE SPREAD (Austro/Hungarian specialty)

½	pound farmer cheese or goat cheese
3	tablespoons butter
2	tablespoons sour cream
3	tablespoons finely chopped onion
1	tablespoon vinegar pickles, finely chopped
1	teaspoon capers, finely chopped
1	teaspoon prepared mustard
1	teaspoon anchovy paste or 2 mashed anchovy filets
2	teaspoons paprika
2	tablespoons caraway seeds

Press the farmer cheese through a fine sieve, add all of the ingredients, and blend them well into a smooth paste. Refrigerate the spread for 1 hour before serving. Garnish with chives or olives.

SALMON MOUSSE (Austrian specialty)

Serves 6

1	can pink salmon (18 ounces)
1	packet unflavored gelatin
¼	cup cold water
½	cup boiling water
½	cup mayonnaise
1	tablespoon lemon juice
1	tablespoon chopped scallions
½	teaspoon salt
¼	pound smoked salmon
¼	teaspoon white pepper
½	cup heavy whipping cream
1	tablespoon chopped capers
2	egg whites stiffly beaten

Dissolve the gelatin in the cold water. Add the boiling water and stir well. In a deep bowl, mix the dissolved gelatin, mayonnaise, scallions, lemon juice, salt, and pepper. Drain the canned salmon. Cut the smoked salmon into small pieces and place all of the above in a food processor. Puree the mixture and transfer into a bowl. Whip the cream, beat the egg whites to a stiff peak, and fold both carefully into the mixture. Oil a fish mold (or any other mold) and fill it with the mousse. Refrigerate it overnight. Before serving, unfold the mousse by inverting the mold onto a serving platter and placing a hot towel over it. Decorate the dish with hard-boiled eggs or with red caviar.

STUFFED EGGSHELLS (My mother's recipe)

Since the age of ten, I have never ever eaten these eggs anywhere else. I did not have a recipe, but I reconstructed the composition and technique based on gustatory memory. To my great surprise, my relatives and friends, who also remembered it from their homes, approved the result.

Serves 8

8	eggs
1	large onion
4	tablespoons vegetable oil
	salt and pepper to taste

Put the eggs in cold water and boil for 10 minutes on medium heat. Rinse them immediately with cold water. With a very sharp and thin knife, cut the eggs lengthwise and carefully scoop out the hard-boiled yolk and white. Set aside the halved shells. Finely chop the onion and sauté in hot oil until light brown. With a fork, mash the hard-boiled eggs, add the onion, and salt and pepper to taste. With a spoon, fill the half shells and smoothen the top. In a large skillet, heat the oil and fry the stuffed half-egg shells for a few minutes until light brown. Serve as an appetizer.

Cooking Tip:
Grapefruit spoons are best for handling the stuffed egg shells, but regular teaspoons will do the job as well.

VEGETARIAN CHOPPED LIVER

Serves 12

6	eggs hard-boiled
1	cup walnuts
16	ounces peas (canned)
2	onions

Sauté the finely chopped onions. Grind everything in a food processor. Add salt and pepper to taste.

SALADS

BEET SALAD

Serves 4

4	small beets
2	eggs
2	medium dill pickles
1	small red onion
½	small herring (matjes)

Boil fresh beets in salted water until they are tender. Cool and peel. Cube the beets. Boil the eggs for six minutes, rinse with cold water, peel and cube. Chop the onion, pickles, and herring. Season them with salt and pepper. Mix well and serve.

BEET SALAD (Bulgarian style)

Serves 4

1	(14.5 ounces) can sliced or shredded cooked beets
2	tablespoons lemon juice
½	teaspoon salt
¼	cup plain yogurt

Mix all of the ingredients, and let them chill for one hour.

BLACK RADISH SALAD (Bukovina style)

Serves 4

1	medium black radish grated
1	small mild onion grated
2–3	tablespoons olive oil
1–2	teaspoon white vinegar
	salt and pepper to taste

Mix all of the ingredients, adjust seasoning, and cover tightly, as this dish emits a pungent odor.

Cooking Tip:
Other radishes, like the violet winter radish or small red radish, can be used as well

CARROT SALAD (Martha Vida)

Serves 4

4	carrots
1	teaspoon mayonnaise
1	teaspoon sour cream
⅓	of a banana
¼	green pepper
1	clove garlic
1	teaspoon lemon juice
1	teaspoon oil
1	dash salt
1	dash sugar

Cut the banana into small cubes, and sprinkle it with lemon juice. Grate the carrots; add the sugar, salt, lemon juice, pepper and remaining ingredients. Add the banana cubes, toss and serve chilled.

Cooking Tips:
You can substitute banana with pineapple.
The same recipe is good for beets by adding some fresh horseradish and caraway seeds, instead of banana.

CELERIAC SALAD (Celery root)

Serves 4

1	pound celeriac
4	tablespoons white vinegar
8	tablespoons vegetable oil
½	lemons
1	teaspoon sugar
½	apple grated
¼	teaspoon white pepper
	salt to taste

Peel the celeriac; rinse it and julienne. Place it in a pot; add salt, sugar, and lemon juice, and barely cover with water. Boil covered on low heat until the celeriac is al dente. Let it cool in its own liquid. Remove it from the pot; drain and add the grated apple. Season with the salt, oil, and vinegar. Serve chilled.

CUCUMBER SALAD (Transylvanian style)

Serves 8

3	seedless long cucumbers or 6 medium cucumbers
2	tablespoons salt
2	tablespoons sour cream
3	tablespoons mayonnaise
1	medium onion finely chopped
3	large garlic cloves pressed
4	teaspoons olive oil
1	dash sugar
1	tablespoon fresh minced dill weed
1	tablespoon white vinegar
	salt and pepper to taste

Peel and slice the cucumbers very thinly. Sprinkle them with salt; mix and let them stand for two to three hours. Squeeze out all of the liquid through a cheesecloth. In a large salad bowl, mix all of the remaining ingredients and adjust the seasoning. Serve chilled.

EGGPLANT SALAD (Romanian specialty)

Serves 6

3	eggplants
1	onion
8	tablespoons vegetable oil
3	tablespoons white vinegar
1	tablespoon salt
2	teaspoons liquid smoke

The best way to prepare the eggplants is to grill them on charcoal. If that is not possible, broil them until the skin is burnt on all sides. To conserve the light color, peel the burnt skin while still hot by letting the cold water faucet run, in order to wet your fingers during the peeling.

Place the eggplants on a plastic or wooden board, and slice them open with a wooden spoon or spatula; discard most of the seeds. Place the board in a slightly vertical position to let excess liquid run out.

If done the old-fashioned way:

Cut the eggplant into very small pieces and put them into a wooden salad bowl, or just leave them on the wooden board. Mix them with the wooden spoon, gradually adding the oil until the eggplant mixture is smooth and foamy. The more you mix, the lighter the color will be. If you do it on the board, just chop and mix while adding the oil.

Chop the onion and add to the eggplant mixture together with the vinegar and salt. Refrigerate it and serve later on a platter; decorate with tomatoes and green peppers, or whatever your desire.

In an electric mixer:

Mix on low speed, adding the oil gradually to a smooth and foamy consistency. Transfer the mixture into a nonmetallic bowl, and add all the other ingredients. Mix well.

If it is not done on a grill, add the liquid smoke to give it the charcoal flavor.

Cooking Tips: Serve with any dark bread. It can be kept refrigerated for one week.
Buy medium, spongy, light eggplants.
Use only white or yellow onion.

EGGPLANT SALAD (Israeli style)

Serves 6

2	large eggplants
1	tablespoon tomato paste
1	cube chicken bouillon
⅓	cup water
½	teaspoon cumin seed
½	tablespoon garlic
⅓	cup vinegar
½	teaspoon sugar
1	tablespoon parsley

Partially peel the eggplants; slice them and salt. Leave them overnight. The next day, drain and pat them dry with paper towels. Cube them and deep fry until they are golden brown.

For the sauce, boil the remaining ingredients for two minutes. Cool it and mix in the fried eggplant. Store the mixture in a tightly closed jar. It can be kept refrigerated for four weeks

EXOTIC SALAD

Serves 12

½	white cabbage shredded
4	medium carrots peeled and shredded
1½	cups mayonnaise
4	slices canned pineapple cubed
1	dash sugar
½	cup peeled and toasted almonds for garnish
	white vinegar, salt, and pepper to taste

Mix all of the ingredients, and let them chill for one hour. Before serving, sprinkle the salad with toasted almonds.

ISRAELI SALAD

Serves 6

4	large, ripe, firm tomatoes
1	red bell pepper
1	green bell pepper
4–5	Israeli cucumbers, unpeeled (or 1 long, seedless)
2	tablespoons chopped parsley

For the dressing

3	tablespoons sunflower or any vegetable oil
1	tablespoon olive oil
1	tablespoon wine vinegar
1	tablespoon lemon juice
1	large crushed garlic clove
1	teaspoon salt
½	teaspoon black pepper
1	teaspoon confectioners' sugar

If you have a "vegetable chop and measure" tool, this salad will be ready in minutes. Half the peppers and discard the seeds and the white pith. Don't peel the cucumbers. Dice all of the vegetables by hand or by tool into even small cubes.

For the dressing, whisk together all of the ingredients, except the parsley. Pour this over the vegetables and stir in the chopped parsley; adjust the seasoning and serve it cool but not chilled.

MARINATED FENNEL SALAD

Serves 4

1	fennel bulb raw
2	tablespoons lemon juice
2	tablespoons fennel leaves
4	tablespoons olive oil
½	tablespoon oregano
1	clove garlic
2	tablespoons parmesan cheese
1	pinch sugar

Remove the fennel stalks and cut off the feathery leaves. Discard the stalks, but save the leaves. Very thinly slice the fennel bulb in a food processor, or grate it by hand. Place it in a glass or porcelain dish, and toss it with lemon juice. Let it marinate for 20 minutes. Wash and chop the reserved leaves, and toss them with the fennel. Add the olive oil and all of the other spices. Add salt and pepper to taste. It is best when served cold.

MUSHROOM SALAD

Serves 6

1	pound mushrooms
2	tablespoons mayonnaise
2	tablespoons club soda
½	teaspoon mustard
2	tablespoons sour cream
1	teaspoon dill weed
2	cloves garlic
1	teaspoon lemon juice
1	medium onion
1	teaspoon white vinegar
2	teaspoons vegetable oil
	salt and pepper to taste

Wash and peel the mushrooms, and cover them with ice water, adding some lemon juice to preserve the white color. Finely chop the onion. Dissolve the mayonnaise by gradually whisking in the club soda. Add all of the ingredients except the dill.

Rinse and pat dry the mushrooms and slice thinly. (Stems can be used too.) Mix them carefully with the dressing, and sprinkle the dill on top. Serve chilled.

POTATO SALAD

Serves 4

2   pounds potatoes

Dressing:

6   tablespoons vegetable oil
2   tablespoons cider vinegar
1   large mild onion chopped
3   tablespoons chopped parsley
1   teaspoon mustard
1   large pickled dill cucumber minced
1   green pepper chopped
2   hard boiled eggs sliced for garnish
      salt and pepper to taste

Wash and boil the potatoes in their skin in salted water until they are tender. Peel them while they are warm and slice or cube them. Place sliced potatoes into a bowl. Mix well all the dressing ingredients and pour over the still-warm potatoes and toss well. Garnish with the egg slices.

ROASTED BELL PEPPERS

Serves 8

3	green bell peppers
3	red bell peppers
½	cup vegetable or olive oil
3	cloves crushed garlic
1	teaspoon sugar
¼	cup white vinegar
¼	cup water
	salt and pepper to taste

Preheat the oven to 375°F. Wash the peppers, and pat them dry. Place the peppers on a baking sheet under the broiler, about 3½ inches away from the heat; or roast them in the oven at 400°F until they are soft and the skin blackens. During the baking or broiling, the peppers have to be turned once.

Put the hot peppers into a brown paper bag and twist it closed or in a pan with a tight-fitting lid for about 15 minutes. This makes peeling the skin much easier. (See tips for peeling.) Let them cool, peel them, and remove the stems and the seeds. I like to keep the juice for the dressing, but first it needs to be strained.

Slice the pepper into halves or into quarter-inch long strips, and place them in a large jar. Combine the remaining ingredients for the dressing; mix well and strain before pouring it into the jar. Shake it several times to combine all of the ingredients and to cover the peppers well. Close the jar tightly and refrigerate it. From time to time, shake the jar, and do the same before serving.

RUSSIAN BEET SALAD

Serves 6

1	pound beets or 3–4 medium beets
3	medium potatoes, peeled and diced
3	carrots coarsely diced
1	onion finely chopped
2	dill pickles diced
3	scallions finely chopped
1	cup cooked green peas, or 18 ounces canned and drained
2	hard-boiled eggs diced

For the dressing

⅓	cup olive oil
2	tablespoons red vine vinegar
1	teaspoon sugar
1	teaspoon dry mustard

Clean the beets, cut off the ends, and cook them in a pressure cooker for 25 minutes or on the stove for about one hour. Peel and dice them into small cubes.

Cook the carrots, potatoes, and peas until they are tender. Dice all of the vegetables to the same size as the beets. Place all of the vegetables and diced eggs in a deep salad bowl and combine them with the dressing (combine all of the dressing ingredients), which has been mixed well with a wire whisk. Add salt and pepper to taste and mix well. Cover and chill the salad for a few hours before serving. Serve on a bed of lettuce, garnished with springs of parsley.

Cooking Tip:
If you are in a hurry, you can use canned beets, carrots, and peas, but not potatoes.

TOMATO SALAD

Serves 6

4	large ripe tomatoes
1	medium onion finely chopped
2	tablespoons chopped parsley
¼	teaspoon sugar
3	tablespoons olive oil or vegetable oil
2	tablespoons white vinegar
1	green bell pepper

Wash and dice the tomatoes and peppers. If so desired, place the tomatoes into boiling water for a few seconds and peel them before dicing. Add all of the remaining ingredients and toss them lightly. Chill for one to two hours before serving.

Cooking Tip:
To give the salad an Italian flavor, add some basil, thyme, and oregano.

TUNA SALAD

Serves 4

1	can tuna
2	hard-boiled eggs
2	tablespoons mayonnaise
1	small onion
2	stalks celery
2	teaspoons mustard seed
1	tablespoon lemon juice
2	drops hot sauce
¼	teaspoon curry powder
1	tablespoon oil
	salt and pepper to taste

Drain the tuna and flake it well. Finely chop the onion and mix all the ingredients well.

TURKISH SALAD

Serves 8

3	medium eggplants
⅓	cup vegetable oil
4	cloves garlic
⅓	cup white vinegar
5	ounces tomato juice
⅓	cup ketchup
½	green bell pepper chopped
1	onion chopped
1	dill pickle chopped
½	red bell pepper chopped
¼	cup water
1	dash sugar
	salt and pepper to taste

Always buy spongy, light eggplants. Peel them only partially and slice them finger-thick. Sprinkle them with salt, and leave them for a few hours. Squeeze out the liquid and blot them dry with a paper towel. Oil or line two baking sheets with parchment paper, and put the eggplant slices to broil on both sides. Let them cool and cut them into small cubes. Whisk the oil, vinegar, water, tomato juice, ketchup, sugar, onion, garlic, salt, and pepper, and pour it over the eggplant cubes. Add the chopped peppers, adjust the seasoning, and mix well. Cover it and refrigerate overnight. Mix several times before serving.

ZUCCHINI CARROT SALAD (Romanian specialty)

Serves 6

5	zucchinis
3	carrots
2	tablespoons dill weed
2	tablespoons parsley
2	tablespoons scallions
4	tablespoons vegetable oil
3	tablespoons lemon juice (or vinegar)
	salt and pepper to taste

Use young and thin zucchinis as well as young carrots. Peel the carrots, but do not peel the zucchinis. Grate both of them on the large side of a grater. Mince the scallions, parsley, and dill weed. Mix all of the ingredients; add salt and pepper to taste and serve it chilled.

SOUPS

AJIACO (Colombian soup)

Serves 8

1	(3 pounds) chicken or chicken breasts
6	quarts water
3	pounds russet potatoes
3	pounds white potatoes
3	pounds "papa criolla" (or Baby Dutch Yellow potatoes)
4	ears corn (not sweet)
1½	tablespoons "quascas"
3	tablespoons capers
3	tablespoons cilantro leaves
1	cup sour cream
2	tablespoons salt
1	carrot
1	onion
3	stalks celery
4	ripe avocados

Cut corn into 3"pieces. Clean and cut the chicken into 8 portions. Cook the chicken in water with the salt, corn, and soup greens like a regular chicken soup. When the meat is tender, discard the soup greens, save the corn, remove the chicken, and set it aside. Once the chicken is cool enough to handle, remove the skin and cut it into strips.

Add the potatoes and bring them to a boil. Reduce the heat, and simmer covered until the potatoes are done. Add the chicken pieces, corn, capers, cilantro, and quascas, and cook for another 5 minutes.

Serve it in deep bowls, making sure that each has some chicken and a piece of corn. You can garnish with a tablespoon of sour cream, but I love to mix the cream into the soup before serving it. Avocados are served in a separate dish so that your guests have the choice of cutting and adding them to the soup or eating them separately.

Cooking Tips:

Quascas and Papa criolla can be found in Latin supermarkets. The potato comes in cans or frozen. To substitute, use Dutch Creamer, Baby Dutch Yellow, or Yukon gold potatoes. The "Papa Criolla" is supposed to break up in the soup to make it thicker and give it the yellowish color. The quascas come in small plastic bags like dried leaves.

MUSHROOM AND BARLEY SOUP

Serves 6

⅔	cup barley
3	cups beef broth
½	cup water
3	tablespoons butter
1	large onion
2	carrots
2	ribs celery
2	potatoes
½	pound mushrooms
¼	teaspoon thyme
2	cups green beans
½	cup parsley (or dill)
3	tablespoons sour cream
	salt and pepper to taste

Wash and drain the barley. In a large stockpot, combine the beef with the barley and cook until it is almost done. Grate the onion on the large side of the grater. Peel the carrots and celery, and grate them as well. Cook the green beans in salted water; drain and slice. Rinse and slice the mushrooms. Peel and cut the potatoes into small cubes.

In a large skillet, heat the butter and sauté the onions and carrots, and then the celery and mushrooms. Add the potatoes, the thyme and the sautéed vegetables. Add salt and pepper to taste. Add the green beans.

In a small bowl, mix the sour cream with some of the broth, and add it to the soup. Bring the soup to a boil, and quickly remove it from the stove. Serve the soup with chopped parsley. If the soup is too thick, add more beef broth.

(Beef broth can be substituted with 2 cubes of beef bouillon dissolved in 3 cups of water)

BEEF CONSOMME (Rindsuppe)
With Boiled Beef

Serves 7

4	quarts water
3	pounds flanken or short ribs
1	pound oxtails or knuckle bones
1	onion with skin
3	carrots
2	parsnips
1	turnip
1	leek
3	celery stalks
1	parsley root
1	green bell pepper
10	peppercorns
1½	tablespoons salt
1	tomato
1	bunch parsley
1	bunch dill weed

Rinse the bones and beef. In a large pot, bring the water to a boil, and add the flanken with the bones. Cook for a few minutes, reduce the heat, and skim the foam every 3-5 minutes for the next 30 minutes. Peel and cut the vegetables in halves or quarters, and add them to the beef together with the salt and pepper. Cover the soup and simmer for 2-3 hours, depending on the quality of the beef. Remove the vegetables, peppercorns, and the bones. Adjust the seasoning, let the broth cool completely, and refrigerate it overnight. If the soup is not clear, strain it through double cheesecloth inside a sieve. The next day, remove the fat that formed on top of the soup. Serve the boiled beef with either horseradish or mustard.

Cooking Tip:
An excellent taste is achieved by first sautéing the vegetables in hot oil until they are brownish, and then adding the water and the beef.

BLACK BEAN SOUP

Serves 6

1	tablespoon extra virgin olive oil
1	onion
3	cloves garlic
1	pound can black beans, drained and rinsed
½	teaspoon cumin powder
1	tablespoon lemon juice
½	teaspoon dried oregano
2	tablespoons finely chopped parsley
4	cups water
¾	cup sour cream
2	teaspoons salt
4	green onions
	pepper to taste

Finely chop the onion, and sauté it on moderate heat until it is translucent, 3-4 minutes. Add the mashed garlic and sauté it until the onion is slightly golden, another 3-4 minutes. Drain and rinse the beans. Set aside a few tablespoons of beans to be mashed with a potato masher. Mix all of the ingredients into the water, add the mashed beans, cover, and simmer for 10 minutes. Serve the soup hot topped with one or two of the optional toppings (sour cream or thinly sliced green onions).

BORSCHT COLD (Jewish specialty)

Serves 6

2	pounds red beets
2	tablespoons sugar
1	lemon
6	red potatoes
1	cup sour cream
	salt and pepper to taste

Peel and dice the beets. Put them to boil in about eight cups of water with salt and pepper, and let them simmer covered for about 1½ hours, or until the beets are soft. Let the soup cool, and then refrigerate. Before serving, add the lemon juice and sugar. Serve with a boiled potato and sour cream. For a clear soup, remove the beets and use them for a salad.

BROWN POTATO SOUP

Serves 6

4	potatoes
1	onion
1	carrot
2	cloves garlic
½	cup all-purpose flour
2	cubes beef bouillon
¼	cup pasta (Orzo or flakes)
2	tablespoons vegetable oil

Finely grind the onion and carrot, and sauté in them oil until they are limp. Peel and cube the potatoes. Fill a pot with water; add the bouillon cubes, salt and pepper, as well as the sautéed onion and carrot. Add the crushed garlic. When the potatoes are cooked, make a roux by frying the flour in a saucepan without oil until it is light brown. Add cold water and stir it until it is smooth, and then add it to the soup. Small pasta flakes or orzo may be added.

CHICKEN SOUP (Jewish Penicillin)

This soup can be served with thin egg noodles, cooked separately and well rinsed, as well as with matzo balls or rice.

Serves 8

1	(5 pounds) large chicken
1	pound necks and wings
2	large onions yellow
2	carrots
1	leek
1	turnip
3	stalks celery
1	medium rutabaga
1	large parsley root
1	potato
½	green pepper
1½	tablespoons salt
1	teaspoon whole peppercorns
1	parsnip
1	bunch parsley
1	bunch dill

Cut the chicken into 8 portions. Wash and clean the necks and wings, and place them together with the chicken pieces in a large pot with 9 cups of cold water. Add the peeled vegetables, peppercorns and salt. Do not peel the onions; just cut off the ends and rinse. (The skin will give the soup more color.) Cover the pot and bring to a boil. Uncover and reduce the heat, while removing any scum. Partially cover and simmer on low heat for about 1–1½ hours. Rinse the parsley and dill under the faucet and tie them with a kitchen twine. Rub in some salt and drop them into the soup for the last 5 minutes before removing from heat.

Remove the chicken and set it aside. Discard the wings, necks, and onions. Reserve the remaining vegetables. Strain the soup if necessary and return the chicken pieces to the broth. Correct the seasoning.

Cooking Tips
The soup vegetables can be used: well-drained for vegetable patties (see recipe); cubed and served in the soup; or as a cold side dish mixed with a salad dressing.

COLD POTATO SOUP (Czernowitz specialty)

Serves 6

4	white potatoes
1	medium onion
1	carrot
2	eggs
½	cup thin noodles
½	cup sour cream
1	tablespoon dill weed
1	tablespoon parsley
1	tablespoon salt

Bring the water, salt, potatoes, onion, and carrot to a boil. Lower the heat; cover and simmer until the potatoes are almost done. Add the noodles. Wash the dill and parsley, and tie them with a cooking twine. Add them to the soup.

When the noodles and potatoes are done, discard the onion, carrot, and herbs. In a small bowl, whisk the eggs with sour cream and gradually add some of the soup liquid, continually beating and adding more liquid so that the cream mixture does not curdle. Now pour the cream mixture into the warm soup, and bring it to a boil for just a second.

Cooking Tip:
This soup is traditionally served cold on hot summer days. It can also be served hot, but be careful not to boil it, to prevent curdling.

CREAM OF BROCCOLI SOUP

Serves 6

2	pounds broccoli
1	medium onion
1	potato
1	chicken flavor bouillon cube
¼	teaspoon white pepper
¼	teaspoon garlic powder
¼	teaspoon nutmeg
¼	teaspoon curry powder
2	tablespoons all-purpose flour
2	tablespoons butter
1	cup milk

Cut the broccoli stalks off the flowers, trim the ends and slice into small pieces. Chop the onion; peel and dice the potato. In a heavy pot, melt the butter and sauté the onion until it is light yellow; add flour to make a roux. When the flour is slightly brown, remove it from the heat and mix in the milk, stirring constantly to avoid clumps.

Boil the broccoli and potato in lightly salted water with the chicken bouillon cube until stems are tender. Cool it and then blend in a mixer, half of the amount at the time until it is smooth. Add the soup to the béchamel sauce, and mix it well. Add all of the seasoning and bring it to a boil until it is creamy. Taste and adjust the seasoning if necessary. Add a tablespoon of sour cream to each soup plate before serving.

CREAM OF WHEAT SOUP

Serves 6

6	cups chicken or beef broth
¾	cup cream of wheat
1	egg yolk
1¼	cups mushrooms finely sliced
1	cup milk
4	tablespoons butter
4	tablespoons parsley or chives
¼	teaspoon nutmeg
	salt and pepper to taste

In a large saucepan, melt the butter and lightly sauté the cream of wheat until it is golden brown. Extinguish it with the hot boiling broth, add the mushrooms, and simmer until both the cream of wheat and the mushrooms are done. Remove from heat and incorporate the beaten egg yolk; add the parsley and nutmeg and rectify the seasoning.

Cooking Tip:
This is a soup that can be quickly prepared in case of unexpected company. Use canned mushrooms, dissolve beef bouillon cubes to make the broth, and use the quick-cooking cream of wheat.

GOULASH SOUP (Austro-Hungarian specialty)

This soup is traditionally served on New Years' Eve.

Serves 6

1½	cups chopped onions
½	pound cubed beef
1	cup cubed potatoes
2	tablespoons vegetable oil
½	teaspoon sweet paprika
8	cups beef broth (or water)
1	teaspoon tomato paste
2	pressed garlic cloves
1	teaspoon white vinegar
½	teaspoon caraway seeds powder

In a deep frying pan, heat the oil and sauté the onions to a golden yellow color. Add the beef; stir and add the paprika. Sprinkle it with the vinegar; add the tomato paste and spices, and pour in the broth. Simmer covered on medium heat for about 40 minutes. Add the potatoes and simmer until they are soft.

Cooking Tip:
If a thicker soup is desired, dissolve a tablespoon of flour in some cold water and add it to the soup, letting it come to a boil.

GREEN PEA SOUP

Serves 6

8½	cups water
½	pound green peas
2	tablespoons barley
1	large onion
1	carrot
2	stalks celery
2	cubes beef bouillon
1	tablespoon vegetable oil
1	tablespoon all-purpose flour
1	tablespoon parsley
1	tablespoon dill

Chop the onion and sauté it in the hot oil until it is transparent. Grate the carrot and celery, and sauté for 5 minutes, continuously scraping the bottom of the pan. Sprinkle them with flour and continue stirring it for another couple of minutes.

In a large pot, bring the water to a boil and add the beef cubes, peas, barley, and sautéed vegetables. Cook for about 45 minutes or until the peas and the barley is tender. Tie the parsley with kitchen twine and add it to the soup just before turning off the heat. Remove the parsley, add the chopped dill, and adjust the seasoning.

HUNGARIAN CABBAGE SOUP

Serves 8

1	cup shredded sauerkraut
2	large onions
½	teaspoon sweet paprika
⅓	cup bacon
½	cup smoked meat (optional)
4	hot dogs
2	large potatoes
2	tablespoons tomato paste
1	cube beef bouillon
6½	cups water
2–3	cloves garlic minced
¼	cup sour cream
1	tablespoon caraway seeds

Rinse sauerkraut. Bring the water to a boil, add the beef cube, sauerkraut, tomato paste, garlic and caraway seeds and simmer on low heat.

Finely chop the onion and bacon, and sauté them lightly. Add the paprika and mix it with the broth. Peel and finely grate the potatoes, and add them to the soup when the cabbage is almost done. Cook for 5 more minutes.

When the cabbage is soft, add the smoked meat and the sliced hot dogs. Add salt if needed.

Cooking Tips:
When a creamier consistency is desired, mix two tablespoons of flour with the sour cream and slowly add it to the soup. Sour cream can be mixed in before serving or added at the table

The same soup can be made with half the amount of fresh cabbage and half the amount of sauerkraut.

PINTO BEAN SOUP

Serves 6

½	pound pinto beans
2	tablespoons vegetable oil
1	large onion finely chopped
1	large carrot chopped
3	celery stalks finely chopped
2	cubes beef bouillon
1	tablespoon all-purpose flour
5	garlic cloves pressed
1	bunch parsley
1	tablespoon sugar
1	bay leaf
4	tablespoons small egg bow pasta
5	cups water
	salt and pepper to taste

Wash the pinto beans several times, and soak them overnight in the 5 cups of water. The next day, cook them in the same water, adding the sugar, bay leaf, beef cubes, and salt to taste.

In a large skillet, sauté the onion in the oil until it is transparent. Add the carrots and continue to sauté for a few minutes, and then add the celery and mix it well. Add the mixture to the boiling beans. Cover the pot and boil it on medium heat until the beans are almost done. Add the noodles and boil for another 10 minutes.

Separately, sauté the garlic in one tablespoon oil, reduce the heat, and add the flour. Stir it until it acquires a golden color. Remove it from stove and pour in a few ladles of the soup liquid, stirring well until it is creamy. Add to the soup together with the bunch of parsley and let it boil for a minute or two. Remove the parsley, adjust the seasoning.

ROMANIAN SOUR MEATBALL SOUP
(Ciorbâ de Perisoare)

Serves 6

For the soup

8	cups beef broth
2	tablespoons vegetable oil
2	large carrots grated
2–3	parsley roots grated
1	large onion chopped
3	ripe tomatoes peeled and chopped
½	teaspoon dill weed
½	teaspoon chopped fresh parsley
2	stalks celery and some leaves
1	red bell pepper diced
½	cups brine of dill pickles, or juice of one lemon.
1	cup sour cream on the side

In the pot you are going to use for the soup, heat the vegetable oil and sauté the onions until they are translucent. Add the celery, (not the leaves), parsley roots, and carrots to the onions, and continue frying them. Add the broth, tomatoes, and red pepper, and boil them until the vegetables are soft. Add the dill weed and celery leaves.

For the meatballs

1	pound ground beef, or turkey
1	onion finely chopped
½	cup rice
1	egg
1	teaspoon dill weed

½   teaspoon salt

½   pepper to taste

1   slice of white bread, or one roll

Cut off the crust of the bread and soak it in water. Rinse the rice.
Squeeze out the liquid from the bread. Mix all the ingredients; form
teaspoon-size balls and drop them into the boiling soup one by one.
Reduce the heat and cover for 20-25 minutes. After the meatballs are
done, add the pickle brine. The soup should taste decidedly sour; if it
does not, add some more brine. Cover and let it rest for ten minutes.
Discard celery leaves. Garnish with the parsley and serve with some
sour cream.

RUSSIAN BORSCHT

Serves 6

1	pound lean beef
2	tablespoons beef bouillon
4	large beets
1	tablespoon salt
1	quart water
2	carrots
2	turnips
1	onion
½	small white cabbage
2	bay leaves
1	green pepper
2	tablespoons white vinegar
1	teaspoon sugar
2	stalks celery
2	tablespoons butter
1	leek
1	(6 ounces) can tomato puree
1	bunch parsley
1	bunch dill
8	tablespoons sour cream
	black pepper to taste

Shred and cook the beets separately with the vinegar to preserve the color. Cube the beef. Dissolve the bouillon in water; add the beef cubes and cook on low heat for 1½ hours, or until they are very tender. Shred the cabbage, carrots, and remaining vegetables. Chop the onion. In a large pan, melt the butter and sauté the onion, cabbage, and all of the vegetables, and let the vegetables simmer covered for 15 minutes. When the meat is tender, add the vegetables to the beef broth. Add sugar, bay leaf, tomato paste, salt, and pepper, and cook it until vegetables are tender. Pour the cooked beets with the liquid into the beef broth mixture and cook them together for a few minutes. Add the parsley and dill bunches. At the table, serve one tablespoon of sour cream per guest.

SOUP EGG DROPS (Eingetropftes)
For chicken or beef broth

Serves 6

1	eggshell full of water
5–6	tablespoons flour
1	dash salt
1	egg

Mix all of the ingredients well, and drop into the boiling soup through a small funnel or with a teaspoon. Cook them for 8 minutes.

SPINACH SOUP

Serves 8

2	pounds fresh spinach (or two 10-oz package frozen spinach, thawed)
4	stalks celery coarsely chopped
2	carrots, peeled and chopped
2	medium onions, finely chopped
4	tablespoons butter
4	cups chicken broth (or 4 chicken bouillon cubes dissolved in 4 cups water)
1½	cup heavy whipping cream
1	teaspoon fresh or dried chervil leaves
4	tablespoons lemon juice
¼	teaspoon white pepper

Optional: chopped chives or parsley for garnish

Thoroughly rinse the spinach and discard any thick stalks. Cook the fresh or frozen spinach in the hot broth for 10 minutes. Drain, reserving the liquid. In a saucepan, sauté celery, carrots and onions in the heated butter 3-5 minutes. Add the chicken broth; remove it from the heat and puree everything together with the cooked spinach in food processor or blender. Bring the mixture to a boil. Reduce the heat, bring to just before simmering and whisk in the cream slowly into the soup. Add the chervil, pepper and lemon juice, and stir well. Taste the soup for salt before serving, as the broth can be very salty. Pour the mixture into soup bowls. Sprinkle with chives or parsley.

TOMATO SOUP

Serves 6

6	medium peeled, ripe tomatoes or canned
1	large onion finely chopped
2	cups chicken broth
1	tablespoon tomato paste
2	tablespoons butter
1	bay leaf
1	tablespoon sugar
½	cup heavy whipping cream or sour cream
½	teaspoon salt
¼	teaspoon pepper
2	tablespoons all-purpose flour
2	tablespoons minced chives or parsley

In a soup pot, melt the butter and sauté the onion until it is transparent. Add the flour and stir until a golden color is acquired. Cut the tomatoes into quarters and put them into a pot with the broth and tomato paste. Add all of the remaining ingredients, and simmer uncovered for about 30 minutes, stirring occasionally.

Strain the soup through a fine sieve, adjust the seasoning, and slowly mix in the sour cream. Serve it topped with chives.

WHITE BEAN SOUP

Serves 6

½	pound white beans
3	tablespoons barley
1	large onion
2	stalks celery
1	carrot
3	cubes chicken bouillon
1	bunch parsley
1	bunch dill
6	dried mushrooms
1	tablespoon vegetable oil
10	cups water

Soak the beans overnight or a few hours before cooking. Soak the mushrooms also for a few hours. Chop the onion and sauté it in the hot oil until it is transparent. Grate the carrot and sauté it with the onion and grated celery.

Heat the water in a large pot. Squeeze out the liquid from the mushrooms and cut them into small pieces. Transfer the sautéed vegetables, mushrooms, bouillon cubes, beans, and barley into the water, and bring it to a boil. Reduce the heat and cook until the beans are tender. Rectify the seasoning, and add the parsley and dill tied with a kitchen twine. Discard the dill and parsley.

COLD YOGURT AND CUCUMBER SOUP
(Bulgarian specialty)

This is a great treat on a hot summer day.

Serves 6

2	large, seedless cucumbers
3	cups plain yogurt
⅔	cup sour cream
4	cloves garlic
2	tablespoons olive oil
½	cup dill weed
6	ice cubes
	salt to taste

Peel and coarsely dice or grate the cucumbers. Sprinkle them with plenty of salt, and leave them to drain for one hour in a colander. Then rinse them and drain again. In a large bowl or soup terrine, beat the yogurt with the sour cream, crushed garlic, olive oil, and dill weed. Stir in the grated cucumbers. Taste and add salt, if needed. Chill the soup and add ice cubes before serving.

VEGETABLES

BAKED GHIVECI (A Romanian dish)

Serves 6

2	medium unpeeled eggplants cubed
2	red bell peppers
2	green bell peppers
6	pitted and cut up black, Greek olives
1/3	cup water
1/3	cup vinegar
1/3	cup olive oil
4	tablespoons ketchup
1	teaspoon salt
1	teaspoon oregano
1	clove pressed garlic
	black pepper to taste

Mix all of the ingredients, and cover them with foil. Bake at 350°F for twenty to thirty minutes. Serve it hot or cold.

BRAISED ARTICHOKES

Serves 12

3	tablespoons lemon juice
6	medium artichokes
2	large onions
4	carrots
4	cloves garlic
1	teaspoon thyme
½	teaspoon pepper
¼	cup extra virgin olive oil
⅔	cup dry white wine
2	cups water
¼	cup flat-leaf parsley
1	tablespoon salt

Fill a large bowl with ice cold water and stir in the lemon juice. Cut the stems of the artichokes, and remove the tough bottom leaves. Cut 1½ inches off the tops of the artichokes. Trim the tops of the remaining leaves with scissors. Soak the artichokes in the lemon water to prevent discoloration.

In a large pot, place the drained artichokes with all the ingredients, except parsley. Partially cover the pot and cook over medium heat for about one hour or until the artichokes are tender. (A leaf will detach easily.) Shake the pot occasionally. Remove the artichokes from the liquid with a slotted spoon or with thongs, and place them upside down on paper towels to drain.

Serve the artichokes in a large shallow bowl; spoon some of the cooked liquid over them. Sprinkle them with parsley and serve at room temperature.

CREAMED SPINACH WITH FRIED EGGS

Serves 4

2	pounds fresh spinach, well rinsed
1	cup water
2	tablespoons cream of wheat
2	cloves pressed garlic
1½	teaspoons salt
2	tablespoons unsalted butter
½	teaspoon freshly ground pepper
⅛	teaspoon nutmeg
¼	cup sour cream
4	eggs

Rinse the spinach thoroughly under running cold water. Cut off the stems and ribs. Bring the water with one teaspoon of salt to a boil. Add the spinach, cover, and simmer for 3-4 minutes. Drain and cool the spinach under cold water, and then squeeze out the excess moisture, reserving some for later. Chop it by hand or in a food processor. In a large skillet, melt the butter; add the spinach, half a teaspoon of salt, garlic, nutmeg, cream of wheat, and pepper. Continue cooking, stirring all the time until the cream of wheat is done. If necessary, add some of the spinach water. Adjust the seasoning and slowly mix in the sour cream. Fry the eggs sunny side up. Transfer the creamed spinach onto a serving plate, and place the fried eggs on top.

Cooking Tip:
Frozen spinach can be used if fresh spinach is not available.

BOILED GHIVECI (Romanian ratatouille)

Serves 8

8	light, green bell peppers
1	eggplant
3	large onions
5	ounces tomato paste
8	ounces ketchup
1	lemon
2	tablespoons sugar
½	cup oil
1	cup water
	salt and pepper to taste

Peel the eggplant, and cut it into small cubes. Cut the peppers into small squares. Fry the onions in oil until they are golden brown and remove. In the same pan, fry the eggplant and the peppers lightly. Add the tomato paste, ketchup, water, lemon juice, salt, pepper, and sugar. Continue simmering for twenty minutes. Add a few drops of hot sauce.

Cooking Tip:
This can be served as a cold appetizer and as a hot side dish.

STRING BEANS (Victoria Mitrani)

Serves 4

1	pound string beans
1	tomato cubed
2	onions chopped
1	tablespoon olive oil
½	teaspoon sugar
½	teaspoon salt
½	teaspoon pepper
1	tablespoon lemon juice
3	chicken wings (or ½ cube chicken bouillon)

Remove strings from the beans if necessary, top and tail but don't cut them. Sauté the onions in the olive oil to a light brown color. Add the tomatoes, and sauté them for another 5 minutes. Cover the string beans with water; add the chicken wings plus all of the other ingredients. Cover and cook on low heat until they are soft. Discard the wings.

Cooking tip: Instead of chicken wings, I dissolve ½ a chicken bouillon cube in very little hot water and add it to the beans. Omit the salt.

STRING BEANS (Vienna style)

Serves 6

2	pounds green beans
1	onion
3	tablespoons dill
3	tablespoons butter
3	tablespoons all-purpose flour
½	tablespoon sugar
2	tablespoons parsley
1	small lemon
½	cup beef stock
1	cup heavy whipping cream

Cut off the ends and wash the green beans. Cut them lengthwise, and cook them quickly in salty water. Finely chop the onion, parsley, and dill, and sauté them in the butter. Add the flour and pour in some beef stock, and simmer for a few minutes. (The sauce should be thick.) Add the beans, sugar, lemon juice, and salt and pepper to taste. At the very end, add the cream and bring it to a quick boil.

VEGETABLE PATTIES (Gemüse Schnitzel)

Serves 8

1	large potato
2	carrots
4	stalks celery
½	head cauliflower
½	cup green peas
½	cup champignons
½	cup string beans
3	eggs
1	cup plain breadcrumbs
½	cup vegetable oil
½	teaspoon nutmeg

Peel and cube all of the vegetables. Cook the vegetables in salted water until they are almost done. Drain them well, and put them in a cheese cloth to squeeze out all of the liquid. Chop coarsely by hand or in food processor. (Do not puree) Incorporate the eggs, nutmeg, pepper, and salt, and mix well. Refrigerate the mix for one to two hours. Form patties, dip them in the breadcrumbs, and fry them in hot oil on both sides.

Cooking Tip:
When you cook a chicken soup, use all of the vegetable for such patties.

ZUCCHINI IN TOMATO SAUCE

Serves 6

1	diced onion
4	cubed zucchini (if the are young, don't peel them)
4	ounces tomato paste
1	teaspoon sugar (or sugar substitute)
	garlic salt and pepper to taste

Sauté the diced onion in a little oil; add the zucchini previously washed and cut into cubes.

In a different dish, mix the tomato paste, salt, garlic, pepper and sugar, and mix them well. Add this to the zucchini, and pour in enough water to cover them. Cook until they are tender.

ZUCCHINI WITH DILL

Serves 4

5	medium zucchinis
4	tablespoons butter
1	tablespoon sugar
1	tablespoon vinegar or lemon juice
½	cup chicken broth
1	tablespoon flour
1	medium onion
1	tablespoon dill
¼	liter sour cream
	salt to taste

Peel and julienne or slice the zucchini; salt them, and let them rest for one hour. Drain the zucchini. Sauté a finely chopped onion in butter, or other shortening. Add the broth, sugar, vinegar, and dill. Add the zucchini and boil them quickly. Taste for salt. Mix the sour cream with the flour and add to the cooked zucchini.

DRESSINGS

DRESSING FOR COLD ASPARAGUS

Serves 6

3	tablespoons mayonnaise
1	tablespoon mustard
3	tablespoons club soda
	pepper, salt, dill weed, and parsley to taste

Mix the mayonnaise with the mustard, and gradually beat in the club soda to achieve a semi-liquid consistency. Add the salt, pepper, dill, and parsley. Pour over the cooked, cold asparagus.

MAYONNAISE

1	large egg yolk, at room temperature
½	teaspoon prepared or dry mustard
1½	teaspoons lemon juice
¼	teaspoon fine salt
¾	cup vegetable oil
¼	teaspoon white pepper
1	dash sugar
1	teaspoon white vinegar

In an electric mixer or food processor, mix the egg yolk with the mustard, salt, pepper and sugar until combined well. Add the oil at first drop by drop, mixing constantly, then in a thin stream until mixture begins to thicken. Whisk in lemon juice and vinegar, then add remaining ½ cup oil in a very slow, thin stream, whisking constantly until well blended.

SALAD DRESSING FOR ANY SALAD

Serves 20

2	tablespoons vinegar
1	teaspoon Dijon mustard
6	tablespoons olive oil
3	black olives (Greek)
1	dash sugar
	salt and pepper to taste

In a glass or porcelain bowl, pour the vinegar, stir in the mustard, add pepper and salt to taste, add the olive oil, the olives, and stir well. If you prefer it creamy, add one ice cube and stir well.

Cooking Tips:
You can also use: Vegetable oil, Worcester sauce, brown sugar, basil, garlic, tarragon, parsley, dill, or any fresh spices can also be used. Basically it is 3:1 parts oil to vinegar.

SAUCE FOR ZUCCHINI AND BROCCOLI

Serves 6

2	tablespoons mayonnaise
1	cup sour cream
¼	onion
2	tablespoons dill weed
½	teaspoon salt

Finely chop the onion and dill. Mix all of the ingredients well and refrigerate them. Serve on any cooked vegetable. To liquefy the sauce, add a few teaspoons of club soda.

SAUCE FOR GEFILTE FISH

Serves 8

2	tablespoons mayonnaise
1	tablespoon lemon juice
1	tablespoon dill weed
1	pinch sugar
	salt and pepper to taste

Mince the dill weed. Mix all of the ingredients to a smooth cream. This can be used for other dishes as well

SOUR CREAM DRESSING

Serves 4

¼	cup vegetable oil
1	cup sour cream or yoghurt
2	cloves garlic
1	teaspoon paprika
½	chopped onion
	salt and pepper to taste

Mix all of the ingredients and use for any salad.

MAIN DISHES

BASIC GROUND BEEF RECIPE

Serves 12-15

1	pound ground pork
1	pound ground beef
4	slices white bread, or 2 large white rolls
1	large onion, chopped
4	tablespoons vegetable oil
2	eggs
1	teaspoon marjoram
3	tablespoons chopped parsley
4	pressed garlic cloves
½	cup breadcrumbs
	salt and pepper to taste

Cut off the crust of the bread slices or rolls, and soak them in water. Sauté the onions in oil until they are golden brown, and set them aside to cool. Squeeze out the water from the soaked bread and mix it together with the ground pork and beef. Add the eggs, onion, and all the other ingredients, and knead the mixture quickly. Should the mixture appear too dry, add some water. Too much handling or leaving the raw mixture for a long time will make the meat tough. It is best to cook it immediately.

Cooking Tip:
This basic mixture is good for beef patties and meatloaves.

BEEF STROGANOFF (Russian specialty)

Serves 8

1	pound beef (preferable tenderloin)
2	large onions
1	cup dried mushrooms or champignons
4	tablespoons butter
1	teaspoon sweet paprika
1	tablespoon vegetable oil
1	cup beef broth
½	teaspoon salt
½	teaspoon pepper
½	cup dry white or red wine
½	teaspoon tomato paste
1	cup sour cream

Cut the beef in thin strips and sprinkle them with salt, paprika, and pepper. In a large skillet, heat the oil with half the amount of butter, and fry half of the beef slightly on both sides. Add the rest of the butter and fry the remaining beef. (Do not fry all of the beef at once.) Remove the fried beef, lower the heat, and in the same butter, sauté the chopped onions, scraping the bottom of the pan, which will add color to the dish.

When the onions turn transparent, add the sliced mushrooms. Continue sautéing for five minutes, constantly scraping the bottom of the pan with a wooden spoon or spatula. Add the fried beef, wine, broth, and tomato paste; cover and simmer on low heat for about 20 minutes, depending on the quality of the beef. Make sure it is tender.

Slowly add the sour cream, and continue simmering uncovered until the sauce is reduced and creamy. Serve with pasta or white rice.

Cooking Tip:
If dry mushrooms are used, they need to be soaked for several hours or overnight. Slice them before sautéing.

BRISKET

Serves 12

2	pounds brisket
1	can cream of mushroom soup
1	packet Lipton onion soup

Mix the undissolved mushroom soup with the onion soup mixture and coat the brisket. Put it in an oven-roasting bag, and refrigerate it for at least twenty-four hours. Follow the roasting bag instructions.

Cooking Tips:
Instead of an oven-roasting bag, heavy foil will do the trick.

Before baking, you can add some mini carrots and small potatoes to the brisket.

CALF'S LIVER WITH ONIONS

Serves 4

1½	lbs. calf's liver
2	large onions
8	tablespoons vegetable oil
4	tablespoons chopped parsley
1	teaspoon marjoram
½	cup flour
	salt and pepper to taste

Carefully remove the thin membrane that covers the liver and cut into ½ - inch thick slices. Lightly pound the liver with a mallet. Sprinkle the slices with salt, pepper and marjoram and dip in the flour.

Heat 4 tablespoons oil in a large skillet. Slice the onions and fry them in the hot oil until light brown. Remove from the skillet onto a paper towel. Heat the remaining oil in another large skillet, add the liver slices and fry them quickly on both sides. The liver should be light pink inside.

Arrange the fried liver slices on a serving platter, top with the fried onions and sprinkle with the chopped parsley. Serve immediately.

GROUND BEEF PATTIES

Serves 12

1	pound basic ground beef recipe
¼	cup oil
½	cup breadcrumbs

With wet hands, form about 8-10 balls. Flatten them with a knife blade, and shape them into oval or round patties. In a large skillet, heat the oil. Dip the patties in the breadcrumbs, and fry them on medium heat until they are brown on both sides. Don't crowd the skillet. Fry a few at a time.

KOTLETS (Russian specialty)

Serves 6

2	pounds ground beef
4	eggs
½	cup water
½	cup matzo meal
4	cloves garlic
1	cube chicken bouillon
1	onion
½	cup breadcrumbs
4	tablespoons margarine
¼	cup vegetable oil
½	teaspoon black pepper
	salt to taste

Finely chop the onion, crush the garlic, and dissolve the chicken cubes in some of the water. Mix all ingredients, gradually adding the water. Refrigerate the mixture for half an hour. On a sheet of foil, spread the breadcrumbs. With wet hands, form oval patties and lightly roll in the crumbs. Heat the oil and fry the patties just for a few minutes on all sides. Arrange them in a baking dish, placing a piece of margarine on top of each patty and covering them with aluminum foil. Bake covered at 350°F for 40 minutes.

Cooking Tips:
Ground beef, veal, and pork can be used in this recipe.
Onion salt can be used instead of fresh onion.
Breadcrumbs can be used instead of matzo meal.

MITITEI
(Romanian ground beef sausages)

Serves 15

1	pound ground beef
6	garlic
½	teaspoon baking soda
½	cup water
1	teaspoon cumin powder
1	tablespoon salt
1	tablespoon pepper
½	teaspoon marjoram
½	teaspoon thyme
½	teaspoon crushed bay leaves

Dissolve the baking soda in the water. Peel and crush the garlic cloves, and add them to the ground beef together with all of the other spices. Work the mixture thoroughly with your hand, mixing for a few minutes. Put it into a plastic bag and refrigerate it for 12 hours.

With wet hands, form small sausages, like hot dogs but shorter and thicker. Arrange them on a wooden or plastic cutting board, and grill them on a very hot fire; turn them frequently.

Serve two mititei per person. They are good with Mamaliga, French fries, or any kind of potato dish. Serve them with mustard and roasted red peppers on the side.

Cooking Tips:
Best results are achieved when combining beef, pork, and lamb.
If you don't have a grill, use the broiler.

WIENER SCHNITZEL (Breaded veal cutlets)

Serves 6

6	veal cutlets
½	cup all-purpose flour
1	teaspoon salt
¼	teaspoon black pepper
2	cups very fine breadcrumbs
2	eggs
1	tablespoon milk
2	cloves pressed garlic (optional)
½	cup vegetable oil

Make sure the veal cutlets are evenly thin. Place each cutlet between two plastic wraps and flatten them with a mallet to about an eighth of an inch thick. Make several small incisions at the edges to prevent them from curling in the hot oil. Mix the flour, salt, and pepper. In a soup bowl, beat the eggs slightly, and if you wish, add the pressed garlic and mix well. Dip the cutlets first in the flour, then in the eggs, and lastly in the breadcrumbs. Press the cutlet lightly into the breadcrumbs and shake off the loose crumbs. In a deep skillet, heat the oil (1¼ inch deep) and brown the cutlets, carefully turning them with tongs. Remove them from the skillet onto paper towels to drain the fat, and also lightly press a paper towel on top of the cutlets. Place them on a heated platter. Garnish with a slice of lemon on top of each schnitzel.

Cooking Tip: The same cutlet can be made with pork, chicken, or turkey breast.

BEEF STEW

Serves 8

3	pounds eye round roast, chuck or tenderloin
2	onions
2	teaspoons salt
1	tablespoon pepper
3	tablespoons oil
2	carrots
1	green pepper
6	cloves garlic
1	tablespoon sweet paprika
6	celery leaves
	water as needed

Peel the onions and carrots and cut them into thick slices. Peel and slice the garlic. Slice the peppers. Pierce the beef with a fork and rub it with salt, pepper, and paprika.

Pour the oil onto the bottom of a pressure cooker. Layer the onions, carrots, and garlic slices at the bottom, and put the beef on top. Cover the beef with the sliced green pepper and some celery leafs (optional). Add water up to a ¼ of the height of the beef. Cook for 45 minutes. Cool the pressure cooker. Open and turn the beef onto other side, scrape the bottom of pressure cooker to prevent vegetables from burning, and continue cooking for another 30 minutes. Cool it and test for tenderness. If the beef is still tough, cook it for another 10 minutes. Remove it from the heat, and let it stand covered until the pot is cool. Place the beef on a cutting board; cool and then slice it with a sharp knife (not serrated). Save some carrot slices for decoration. Put the beef into a baking dish, pour strained juice on top of it, put a slice of carrot on each portion, and heat in the oven before serving it. If preferred, pass vegetables through a strainer and mix them with the liquid to form a thicker gravy.

BROCCOLI AND CHEESE PIE

Serves 8

8	filo pastry sheets
2	pounds fresh broccoli
¼	cup butter
½	cup onions
3	eggs
½	pound feta cheese
½	cup parsley chopped
2	tablespoons fresh dill chopped
½	teaspoon salt
1	dash black pepper
½	cup butter melted

Preheat the oven to 350°F. Remove the pastry sheets from freezer. Let the pastry sheets warm to room temperature according to the directions on label. Wash the broccoli; trim the leaves and stem ends. Split the heavy stalks. With a sharp knife, coarsely chop the stems and flowerets and place them into a large skillet; add a half cup of boiling water and cook over medium heat covered for 5 minutes. Drain well.

In hot butter in a large skillet, sauté the chopped onion, stirring until golden, about 3 minutes. Add the chopped broccoli; sauté for 1 minute, stirring. Remove from the heat.

In a large bowl, beat the eggs slightly. Add the feta cheese, chopped parsley, dill, pepper, salt, and broccoli mixture; mix well.

Line the inside of a 9-inch spring form pan with 6 filo pastry sheets, overlapping the edges. Brush each pastry sheet with melted butter. Pour the filling into the prepared pan. Fold the overlapping edges of pastry sheets over top of the filling. With scissors, cut four nine-inch circles from remaining sheets (for guide use a nine-inch cake pan). Brush each circle with the melted butter, and then layer one over the other on top of the pie.

With scissors cut through the sheets to make eight sections. Pour any remaining butter over top. Place the spring form on a jelly roll pan to catch drippings. Bake for 40-45 minutes, or until the crust is puffy and golden brown. Remove to the rack; cool for 10 minutes.

To serve: Remove the side of the spring form pan. With a sharp knife, cut into the wedges and remove with a pie server. Serve warm.

Cooking Tips:
Broccoli can be substituted with spinach.

Keep pastry sheets covered with damp paper towels.

Use three packages (10-ounce size) of drained, thawed, frozen chopped broccoli, or spinach.

CHEESE ROLL (Romanian specialty)

Serves 12

For the dough

2	cups milk
4	ounces unsalted butter
1⅓	cup all-purpose flour
4	eggs
4	tablespoons sour cream

For the filling

⅔	cup farmer cheese
⅔	cup feta cheese
⅔	cup grated yellow cheese
1	egg
¼	cup chopped dill weed

Bring the milk and butter to a boil; add the flour at once, and remove the pot from the stove and stir vigorously with a wooden spoon. Let it cool and then add the eggs one by one, stirring thoroughly between each addition. Add the sour cream.

Grease and flour a cookie sheet. Spread the mixture on it and bake at 350°F for 30 minutes, or until it is light brown. Wet a large kitchen towel and turn out the baked sheet on the damp towel. Let it cool for 5 minutes.

Mix the cheeses with the egg and the dill. Spread it evenly over the baked sheet, leaving a rim without the filling. Roll the sheet like a strudel almost to the end, folding the rim over like a bandage. Wrap the moist towel over the roll like an envelope. Refrigerate it in a rectangular plate up to 3 days. Before serving, grease an oven-proof serving dish with butter, and bake at 400°F for 30-35 minutes. (The cheeses should be melted) Serve it hot. Cut slices and serve with a salad on the side.

CHICKEN PAPRIKASH
(A popular Transylvanian dish)

Serves 4

1	cut up chicken, or 4 quarters
2	medium onions
2–3	teaspoons sweet Hungarian paprika
1	cup chicken broth
3	tablespoons vegetable oil or butter
1	green pepper sliced
3	tomatoes peeled and chopped
1	teaspoon sugar
¼	lemon juice and zest
2	tablespoons all-purpose flour
1	teaspoon tomato paste
½	cup sour cream (optional)
	salt and pepper to taste

Clean chicken pieces and pat dry. Sprinkle them with salt and pepper, and fry them in oil in a large skillet, turning them over once. Remove the chicken and put it aside. In the same oil, sauté the chopped onions and peppers until they are soft. Add the chopped tomatoes, tomato paste, sugar, salt, and paprika. Add the chicken broth and stir it well. Add a sliver of lemon zest and reserve the juice. Add the chicken pieces; cover them and simmer for about 30 minutes, or until tender. Add a little water if it becomes too dry. Adjust the seasoning with paprika, and salt and pepper to taste. If served with sour cream, remove the chicken from the pot, whisk the flour with the sour cream, and gradually add to the sauce. Let it simmer for 5 minutes. Strain the sauce, add some lemon juice, and put the chicken pieces back to simmer for 1 minute on low heat. Serve with egg noodles, dumplings, or rice.

CHICKEN WITH RICE (Arroz con pollo)

Serves 8

⅓	cup vegetable oil
2	broiler chickens cut up in small pieces
6	cloves garlic
8	ounces tomato paste
1	green bell pepper
1	(12-oz.) can beer
4	ounces green olives
1	ounce capers
½	cup dry white wine
½	teaspoon ground cumin
16	ounces canned green peas
5	cups water
1	bay leaf
1	pinch saffron
½	teaspoon pepper
2	teaspoons salt
2	pounds white rice
1	jar pimientos (7.5 oz.)
2	cups chicken broth

Make a broth by cooking the chickens for 20 minutes. Roll the chicken pieces in crushed garlic. Heat the oil and brown the chicken. Add finely chopped onion and chopped green bell pepper, and continue sautéing. Add chopped pimientos, including the liquid from the can and the liquid from the peas. Add salt and pepper, bay leaf, saffron, capers, cumin, dry wine, broth, tomato paste and beer. Wash and soak the rice. When the chickens are half cooked, add the rice and cover. Cook it over low heat for 20 minutes or until the rice is done. Stir it constantly to prevent sticking. Add the peas and garnish with pimientos and olives.

CHICKEN-LEEK BURGERS

Serves 6

3	pounds leeks
1	pound chicken breast (or turkey breast)
1	egg
1	slice white bread
¼	cup vegetable oil
	white pepper and salt to taste

Soak the bread in water. Cut off the green parts of the leeks. Slice the leeks in half and rinse them well. Boil them in salty water for 10 minutes, and then drain. Grind the leeks together with the chicken. Add the egg, pepper, and salt. Squeeze out the water from the bread and add it to the mixture. Form patties, or oval balls like gefilte fish, and fry in hot oil on all sides.

CHINESE PEPPER STEAK

Serves 4

1	pound flank steak or chuck
3	green peppers cut into slices
2	medium onions
¼	cup soy sauce
¼	cup oil
2	tablespoons cornstarch
1	cup water
1	clove garlic
½	teaspoon ground ginger
2	stalks celery, thinly sliced
2	ripe tomatoes cut in wedges
	salt and pepper to taste

Slice the flank steak into thin strips, across grain and brown it in hot vegetable oil. Taste the meat. If it is not tender, add water gradually, just enough to cover the meat, and simmer for 30-40 to minutes over low heat. Turn the heat up and add the vegetables, except for the tomatoes. Toss until the vegetables are tender crisp, approximately 10 minutes. Add salt and pepper to taste. Dissolve the cornstarch in soy sauce and water; add ginger and garlic. Add this to the beef; stir and cook until thickened. If necessary, add more soy sauce. Mix in the tomatoes and simmer for one minute. Serve with white rice or noodles.

CHINESE FISH (Hannah Muller)

Serves 12

1	pound thick fish fillets
½	cup potato starch (or corn starch, or flour)
1	lemon
½	cup oil

For the sauce

2	medium onions
1	green pepper
2	medium ripe tomatoes
1	cup water
¼-½	cup dark soy sauce
1	teaspoon corn starch
1	tablespoon sugar
2	cloves garlic
	salt and pepper to taste

Use thick fillets of fish like tilapia. Rinse and blot with them paper towels, and do not salt them. Sprinkle the fillets with the juice of one lemon and dip them in the potato starch. Deep fry them in oil until they are brown.

Slice the onions and sauté them until they are transparent. Slice the green pepper and add it to the onions; continue sautéing. Peel the tomatoes; cube or slice them and add them to the onion and pepper. When the vegetables are soft, add one cup of water into which one teaspoon of corn starch and the soy sauce has been dissolved. Add the sugar. Boil the sauce on low heat until it is brown and transparent. Add the fish and two cloves of pressed garlic. Add pepper and salt to taste. Serve with white rice.

CHINESE TUNA PIE (Hannah Muller)

Serves 12

For the dough

½	pound butter
½	pound farmer cheese
2	cups all-purpose flour
1	egg

For the filling

1	onion
3	tablespoons vegetable oil
2	cans tuna in oil
1	cup rice
2	ounces cellophane noodles (optional)
4	tablespoons soy sauce
1	teaspoon black pepper
	salt to taste

Boil the rice as usual. Chop the onion, and sauté it until it is light brown. Cook the cellophane noodles in salty water for 10 minutes and then drain. Drain the tuna. In a bowl, mix the tuna, rice, noodles, onion, soy sauce, pepper, and salt to taste.

In an electric mixer, or food processor, make a soft dough from the butter, cheese, egg and flour. Divide into 2 equal parts.

Line the bottom and sides of a rectangular baking dish (13" X 9") with half of the dough. Fill with the tuna mixture and cover it with the other half and brush with the beaten egg. Pierce the dough with a fork in several places and. sprinkle with sesame seeds. Bake in preheated oven at 350°F until the crust is light brown. You can also cover the filling with stripes like a lattice.

Cooking Tips:
Farmer cheese can be substituted with any dry cottage cheese or ricotta cheese.
If tuna is packed in water, add a few tablespoons of oil to the filling.
A sesame seed topping is optional.

DAIRY FISH (Bukovina style)

Serves 6

2	pounds fish filets
2	onions
½	cup sour cream
3	tablespoons dill
1	cup water
	salt and pepper to taste

Rinse the fish and cut it into small pieces. Peel and slice the onions. Put the fish, onions, pepper, and salt in a pot to boil until the fish is done. Discard half of the liquid. Carefully incorporate the sour cream, the dill and bring the liquid to a quick boil, being careful not to cause the cream to curdle. Serve with mamaliga (polenta) or any other side dish.

DOCTORED-UP GEFILTE FISH

Serves 12

12	patties gefilte fish
4	onions
4	potatoes
5	carrots
1	tablespoon garlic powder
	salt and pepper to taste

Use the bottled or canned gefilte fish with jellied broth. Put the entire contents into a deep baking dish, sprinkle it with lots of black pepper and garlic powder; add the sliced carrots, peeled and chunked potatoes, and chunked yellow onions with the skin so as to color the broth. Bake the fish at 350°F for about 1½ hours. From time to time, baste the fish with the liquid. Discard all of the vegetables except for some nice slices of carrots to put on top of each fishlet. Carefully transfer the fish to a serving platter. Strain the broth and pour it over the patties. Cool and refrigerate the fish if you like the jellied cold style. Same fish can be served warm.

FALSE GEFILTE FISH (Bukovina Style)

Serves 8

For the fishlets

½	lb ground chicken breast or veal
1	egg
1	white roll
3	tablespoons breadcrumbs
	salt and pepper to taste
	sugar to taste

For the stock

2-3	cups water
2	onions
1	carrot
½	cup cold water for sprinkling
	sugar, salt and pepper to taste

Grind the chicken breast. Peel the roll and soak it in water. Squeeze out the water from the roll and mix it with the ground chicken breast, egg, breadcrumbs, pepper, salt, and sugar to taste. Form oval balls.

Peel and slice the onions. Peel and slice the carrot. Bring the water to a boil and cook it with the onions, carrot, pepper, salt, and sugar to taste. When the vegetables are tender, discard and adjust the taste. Drop the balls into the boiling fish stock and simmer for about ½ hour. Make sure to have enough stock to cover the balls. When ready, sprinkle with the cold water to keep balls hard. Refrigerate the balls and serve them cold.

FISH ROLLS (Lori Einhorn)

Serves 6

1	pound fish filets
½	cup smoked salmon
2	cans cream of undissolved mushroom soup
1	lemon
½	cup mushrooms
1	tablespoon dill weed
½	teaspoon salt
½	teaspoon pepper

Use any thin fish filets. Rinse and dry the filets with paper towels. Sprinkle them with lemon juice, salt, and pepper. Cut the salmon into small pieces and divide into as many portions as the number of filets. Place the salmon pieces on the filets and roll them up, securing with a toothpick. Place the rolls in a Pyrex baking dish, cover them with the soups, and bake for 30 minutes in a preheated oven at 350°F. After 25 minutes, top the rolls with sliced, fresh mushrooms and sprinkle with dill weed. Serve with rice or potatoes.

Cooking Tips:
Use filets of gray sole, or any other white fish.
The same rolls can also be filled with flavored spinach.

FISH WITH RATATOUILLE (Bluma Ramler)

Serves 10

2	onions
2	red peppers
4	tomatoes
1	eggplant
1	cup green peas
½	pound green beans
3	carrots
1	tablespoon sugar
2	tablespoons tomato paste
3	tablespoons dill
1	tablespoon lemon juice
½	cup water
¼	cup white vinegar
1	pound firm-fleshed fish
1	tablespoon lemon juice
	salt and pepper to taste

Peel the tomatoes, onions, and the eggplant. Chop the onions and sauté. Cube the remaining vegetables and add them to the sautéing onions. Continue to sauté the vegetables for 5 more minutes. Add sugar, salt and pepper to taste, tomato paste, lemon juice, and chopped dill. Use any firm-fleshed fish, like tilapia, sole, trout, etc.

Spoon the mixture into an 11¾ x 7½ x 1¾ inch baking dish. Arrange the fish filets on top (about 4-5 pieces) and sprinkle them with dill. Pour the water and vinegar over the fish, cover them with foil, and bake at 350°F for 25-30 minutes or until the fish flakes easily when tested with a fork. Serve the fish warm or chilled.

GEFILLTE FISH (A traditional Jewish dish)

Serves 10

Ask the fishmonger to reserve the heads, bones and trimmings for the stock. He may also grind the fish for you. The more whitefish you add, the softer the patties will be

For the stock

4	cups water
2	carrots
1	onion
2	fish heads, bones and trimmings
2	teaspoons salt
2	teaspoons sugar
½	teaspoon white pepper
1	bay leaf
10	cups water

For the fish patties

2	pounds whitefish, carp and pike (or just 2 varieties)
2	onions
3	slices challah
3	eggs
2	teaspoons sugar
	salt and pepper to taste

Slice the onions and the carrots. Put all of the stock ingredients in a saucepan, add enough water to cover the fish heads and bones, and bring to a boil. Remove the scum and continue simmering on low heat for half an hour and taste for salt, pepper, and sugar. (It should not be too sweet.)

Soak the challah slices without the rind in water. Put the onion, quartered, in the food processor with the eggs, salt, sugar, and pepper, and blend to a cream. Pour the mixture into a mixing bowl. Squeeze out the water from the soaked challah and add to the mixture. If not ground by the fishmonger, cut the fish into pieces and process for a few seconds until they are finely chopped. (It should not turn into a paste.) Add the ground fish to the onion mixture and mix very well. Cover and refrigerate for 30-50 minutes.

With wet hands, shape the mixture into oval patties the size of a lemon. Carefully lower them into the fish stock and simmer covered on low heat for about 30 minutes. Cool and then lift out the patties and arrange them in one layer in a deep Pyrex or other serving dish. Pour a little stock over the fish and reduce the rest by boiling it down, and then strain it over the patties. Retrieve the carrot slices and decorate each fishlet with a slice of carrot placed on top.

Refrigerate overnight, by which time a firm aspic will have formed. Serve the fish with horseradish.

HUNGARIAN GOULASH

Serves 6

1	pound beef chuck or top round
1	pound onions
1	tablespoon tomato paste
1	tablespoon sweet paprika (Hungarian)
1	clove garlic
¼	tablespoon caraway seeds
½	tablespoon marjoram
1	inch shaving of lemon zest
1	green pepper
¼	cup vegetable oil
1	cup water
2	bay leaves
1	tablespoon white vinegar
	salt to taste

Cut the beef into one-inch cubes. Crush the garlic. Finely chop the onions, and sauté them in a large, bottom-heavy saucepan or casserole until they are golden brown. Add the garlic and caraway seeds and sauté the mixture for 1-2 minutes. Remove from heat, add paprika and stir until the onions are coated with paprika. Put the saucepan back on medium heat and stir for a few seconds, careful not to burn the paprika. Add the meat cubes and mix them well until all of the pieces are completely coated with the paprika/onion mixture. Add salt, half a cup of water and stir well. Reduce the heat. Add all of the other ingredients and spices. Peel about a one-inch long strip of lemon zest, and add it to the meat. Cover the pot tightly and simmer, adding water as needed and stirring occasionally. Cook for 1½ hours, or until the beef is tender. Add enough water to cover the beef. When it is ready, remove the lemon zest and the bay leaves.

Cooking Tip: Serve the goulash with dumplings or noodles.

JELLIED CARP (Jewish/Polish Style)

Serves 6

1	small carp (3½ lbs.)
2	medium onions
2	large carrots
1	parsley root
2	teaspoons salt
3	teaspoons sugar
½	teaspoon white pepper
2	bay leaves
4	cups water

Clean the carp and cut it into 2½ inch pieces. Peel the parsley root. Slice the carrots and onions. Put the onions at the bottom of the pan. Place the fish head and steaks on top. Add the remaining ingredients. Pour in the water to barely cover the fish. Bring to the boil and remove the scum. Cook it covered on very low heat for 1½–2 hours until the fish is tender. Adjust the seasoning if needed. (Broth should not be too sweet)

Carefully transfer the fish slices to a deep serving dish with the head at the one end. If there is too much stock, reduce by simmering it uncovered, strain and pour it over the fish. Place a nice slice of carrot on top of each steak. Let it cool, cover with plastic wrap, and refrigerate. Serve the next day. A firm jelly should form.

LAMB PILAF (Middle Eastern specialty)

Serves 6

½	pound lean lamb cubes
3	medium ripe tomatoes
1	large onion finely chopped
1	teaspoon salt
½	teaspoon black pepper
2	teaspoons raisins
1½	cups white rice
2	tablespoons fresh parsley, chopped
3	cups beef broth
1	dash saffron
2	teaspoons pignoli (pine nuts)
4	tablespoons butter
1	green pepper

Julienne the green pepper and slice the tomatoes. Wash the rice and set it aside. Heat the butter in a frying pan. Sauté the onion until it is golden brown. Add the beef cubes and brown them on all sides. Add salt, pepper, tomatoes, green pepper, and raisins. Dissolve the saffron in some broth, and add to the rice. Let it simmer for thirty minutes. Add the rice and stir it for 2 minutes. Add the parsley and broth and cover. Add the pignoli at the end. Cook on medium heat for about 30-35 minutes. Stir every 5 minutes.

Cooking Tip:
Lamb can be substituted by beef.

MEATBALLS IN TOMATO SAUCE (Bukovina style)

Serves 6

For the balls

½	pound ground beef (or veal, chicken, or turkey)
1	large onion finely chopped
1	white bread roll (or a Kaiser roll, or a few slices of white bread)
1	tablespoon breadcrumbs
2	eggs
1	dash sugar
2	teaspoons salt
2	tablespoons vegetable oil

For the tomato sauce

5	cups water
1	tablespoon salt
3–4	teaspoons sugar
1	(5 ounces) can tomato paste
1	bay leaf

For the Béchamel sauce (white sauce):

2	tablespoons oil
2	tablespoons all-purpose flour
½	cup cold water, or more

Cut off the crust of the roll and soak it in water. In a large skillet heat the oil and sauté the chopped onion until it is light brown Squeeze out the liquid from the roll and add it to the meat mixture. Mix all of the ingredients well by hand. With wet hands, form small balls of meat and lightly fry them on both sides.

Prepare the tomato sauce by diluting the tomato paste in the water, adding salt, pepper, and sugar to taste. (It should taste sweet/sour.) Drop the meat balls into the boiling sauce. Lower the heat and simmer for half an hour.

For the béchamel sauce:
Heat the oil; add the flour and mix until it is light brown. Quickly add the cold water and continue mixing until it is slightly thickened. Gradually add this to the tomato sauce, making sure no clumps are formed. If needed, strain it. Let it boil for one minute.

Serve with white rice or spaghetti.

MEATLOAF (Lilly Karsai)

Serves 12

2	tablespoons chopped onions
2	cloves pressed garlic
½	pound mushroom pieces
2	pounds ground beef
1	packet puff pastry
1	teaspoon salt
1	teaspoon pepper
2	tablespoons oil
1	egg

Sauté the onion and garlic, and add the mushrooms. Mix the ground beef with pepper and salt to taste. Flatten the beef on a foil or wax sheet, and put the sautéed filling in the center. Roll it like a strudel and bake at 350°F until it is almost done. Take the meat out of oven and cover the top and sides with puff pastry. Brush it with a beaten egg and bake for another 10-15 minutes.

Cooking Tip:
Instead of puff pastry, filo sheets can be used.

CREAMED MUSHROOMS (Bukovina style)

Serves 4

1	pound champignons or any other mushrooms
2	tablespoons butter
1	tablespoon all-purpose flour
1	medium onion
3	tablespoons parsley
½	cup sour cream
2	teaspoon lemon juice
	salt and white pepper to taste

Wash and slice the mushrooms according to their size. Chop the onion and sauté it in a large pan until transparent. Salt and pepper the mushrooms, and add them to the onions, stirring well. Cover the pan, and let it simmer for about 10 minutes until the mushrooms are tender. Discard the surplus liquid. Mix the flour with the sour cream; pour this over the mushrooms, mix well, and simmer uncovered. Add the lemon juice and the parsley. Serve with mamaliga (polenta).

Cooking Tip: The mushrooms can be served as a main dish with mamaliga (polenta) or as a side dish for veal stews.

NOODLE SQUARES WITH CABBAGE (Krautfleckerl)

Serves 6

1	large onion chopped
1	head white cabbage shredded
1	pound noodle squares, or extra wide noodles
2	tablespoons sugar
1	teaspoon vinegar
8	tablespoons vegetable oil or any fat
½	cup beef broth (or water)
	salt and pepper to taste

Salt the shredded cabbage and let it stand for thirty minutes. Press out all of the liquid. Heat the oil in a large skillet and caramelize the sugar. Add and sauté the chopped onion until it is brown. Add the cabbage and vinegar to the skillet and continue sautéing. Add the broth; season it with salt and pepper and simmer until the cabbage is soft.

Cook the noodle squares in salty water and rinse. (If no such ready squares are available, use wide noodles and cut them into one-inch squares.) Mix the noodles with the cabbage, adjust the seasoning, and serve as a main or side dish.

SOY CHICKEN

Serves 4

1	chicken
8	ounces orange juice
2	ounces soy sauce
2	cloves garlic finely minced
½	cup ketchup
¼	cup vegetable oil
	salt and pepper to taste

Cut up the chicken into eight pieces, or use just drums. Mix all the ingredients and pour over the chicken pieces. Marinate for several hours, turning them from time to time. Bake at 400°F for about one hour. Baste with the sauce every 15 minutes.

SPINACH CREPES (Agnes Sapira)

Serves 10

For the crepes

1	cup water
4	eggs
2	cups all-purpose flour
½	teaspoon salt
4	tablespoons oil

For the Bechamel sauce (white sauce)

3	tablespoons all-purpose flour
2	tablespoons butter
2	cups milk
½	cube chicken bouillon
¼	teaspoon pepper
1	cup milk

For the filling

1	onion
1	package Boursin cheese with garlic
10	ounces frozen creamed spinach
8	ounces farmer cheese
2	cloves garlic
	salt and pepper to taste

For the topping

½	cup grated mozzarella cheese

For the crepes

Mix the eggs with the milk, water, oil, melted butter or margarine, salt, and flour in a blender, or beat with a whisk for one minute. Cover and refrigerate the mixture for two hours. Use a lightly oiled seven-inch pan to make twelve crepes.

For the Bechamel sauce

Dissolve the bouillon cube in a few teaspoons of hot milk and add to the cold milk. Melt the butter in a saucepan. Add the flour, stirring continuously for one minute or less over low heat. Add the milk and cook, beating with a whisk, until slightly thickened. Add the pepper.

For the filling

Mix the spinach with the chopped onion, garlic, cheeses, salt, pepper, and half of the béchamel sauce.

Fill the crepes, roll them up, and line them in a greased baking dish. Pour the remaining sauce on top and sprinkle with grated mozzarella cheese Bake at 350° F until the top is light brown. Leftovers can be frozen.

STUFFED CABBAGE (Austrian style)

Serves 10

½	pound ground pork
1	white cabbage
2	white rolls
1	egg
½	cup sour cream
¼	pound smoked bacon slices
1½	cups mushrooms
1	large onion
3½	tablespoons butter
4	tablespoons chopped parsley
1	cup beef broth
	salt and pepper to taste

Blanch the cabbage in boiling water, or put it in the microwave oven for a few minutes until the leaves are soft. Rinse it under cold water and pat dry. Cut out the core, separate the leaves, and cut off the thick ends. Lay the leaves on a flat surface, and then salt and pepper.

Soak the rolls in water, peel of the crust, and squeeze out the liquid. Chop the onion and the mushrooms, and sauté them in the hot butter. Mix the ground pork with the soaked roll, the egg, the sautéed onion, mushrooms, and parsley. Fill each leaf with one tablespoon of meat mixture, roll it up, and tuck in the ends. Place them in a baking dish and cover with bacon slices; pour in the beef broth. Bake at 400°F for 45 minutes. Pour the sour cream over the stuffed cabbage rolls, and bake it for another 15 minutes.

STUFFED CABBAGE JEWISH STYLE

Serves 12

For the stuffing

1	large cabbage (3–4 pounds)
1	pound lean ground beef
½	cup raw white rice
1	egg
1	onion finely chopped
2	tablespoons vegetable oil
1	teaspoon salt
½	teaspoon black pepper
¼	cup ketchup

For the sauce

2	pounds peeled tomatoes, or a 28-ounce can crushed tomatoes
1	teaspoon salt
½	teaspoon black pepper
½	cup ketchup
3–4	tablespoons sugar
2	large onions chopped
1	lemon for juice
2	tablespoons vegetable oil

Sauté the onion in oil until it is transparent, and then combine it with the meat; stir until it changes color. Mix in the rice and all of the other ingredients (except the cabbage).

With a sharp knife, remove the core from one large head of a cabbage and scald it in boiling water for 10-15 minutes or in a microwave for 10 minutes. Remove a few leaves at the time as they wilt, and set them aside. Cool before using. Shave off the thickest part of the hard rib. Reserve some of the reject leaves to line the bottom of the pan.

Put one to two heaping tablespoons of the rice mixture on each leaf at the base end and roll up loosely, tucking in the sides like an envelope. Line the bottom of a large saucepan or Dutch oven with the reject leaves, and place the rolls seam side down. Arrange them so that they fit snuggly. Repeat with another layer.

For the sauce

Sauté the onions until they are transparent. Liquefy the tomatoes. In a large saucepan, combine all of the sauce ingredients, cover, and bring to a boil; reduce the heat and simmer for 30 minutes or until the sauce is thick. Taste the seasoning to achieve a sweet and sour balance.

Pour the sauce slowly over the cabbage rolls and put a small plate on top to keep them from unfolding. Cook over low heat for 2 hours. Make sure to add water to prevent the rolls from drying out or burning. Serve with sour cream.

STUFFED CABBAGE (Ruth's version)

Serves 12

For the sauce

2	pounds ripe tomatoes
3–4	tablespoons tomato paste
½	lemons (juice of)
3–4	tablespoons sugar
4	cups beef broth
1	teaspoon dill

Caramelize the sugar until it is medium brown, and mix it thoroughly with the broth or with the peeled and liquefied tomatoes. (Beef cubes can be used as well if they are dissolved in four cups of water.) Peel and liquefy the tomatoes in a food processor. Mix the tomato paste, tomatoes, dill, lemon juice, and caramelized sugar with the broth and season with salt and pepper to taste.

For the rolls

1	large cabbage
4	medium onions
2	tablespoons vegetable oil
1	pound beef
½	cup white rice
1	tablespoon tomato paste
1	teaspoon chopped dill
3	tablespoons club soda
1	egg
	salt and pepper to taste

Carefully detach the cabbage leaves from the core and soak them in salted boiling water until they are soft, or microwave for 5-6 minutes. Cut off the hard ribs and save 12 leaves.

Sauté the onions until they are light brown and save half of them for the sauce. Mix the meat, rice, half of the sautéed onions, tomato paste, dill, pepper, salt, and egg; gradually add the club soda as you mix. Fill each leaf with two tablespoons of beef mixture at the stem and roll up loosely; tuck in both sides or fold both sides toward the center and roll up.

Line the bottom of a large pot or pan with the discarded and small leaves to prevent the rolls from sticking. Pack the rolls seam side down. Mix the sauce with the remaining onions and pour it over the rolls making sure they are covered with liquid. Put a plate on top to prevent them from unfolding, and let them simmer on low heat for approximately two hours. Check on the liquid from time to time, adding water if necessary. The rolls can also be baked in the oven for three hours.

Another option is to cook the rolls on the stove for 1½ hours, and then transfer them carefully to a Pyrex dish or other baking dish and bake in the oven for ½ hour.

Serve with polenta and sour cream

STUFFED GREEN PEPPERS (Bukovina style)

Serves 8

8	green bell peppers
1	cup sour cream (optional)

For the filling

½	cup cooked rice
1	onion
3	tablespoons oil
1	pound ground beef
4	tablespoons parsley
1	egg
1	clove garlic
	salt and pepper to taste

Chop and fry the onion in the vegetable oil until it is soft. Mix all the ingredients and fill the peppers. Cover with the reserved caps.

For the sauce

4	cups water
1	onion
2	tablespoons oil
1	15-oz.can tomato sauce
2	tablespoons tomato paste
2	tablespoons sweet paprika
3	teaspoons sugar
	salt and pepper to taste

Fry the chopped onion in oil until it is golden. Pour the 4 cups of water into a large saucepan and stir in all the ingredients. Add the fried onion and let it simmer for ten minutes.

To stuff the peppers, cut off a circle around the stalk ends, remove the seeds and membranes. Cut out the stems and reserve the caps. Slightly pierce the bottoms of the peppers with the point of a sharp knife. Replace the caps. Arrange side by side standing up in a baking dish and pour the tomato sauce around them.

Cover with foil and bake in a preheated oven at 375°F for 1–1½ hours, or until the peppers are soft. Be careful that they do not fall apart and remove them from the oven before they start to. Serve hot.

Cooking Tips:
Different meats or a combination of various ground beefs can be used.
Red, yellow, or a combination of peppers can be used as well.
Instead of baking, the peppers can be simmered on the stove, adding water as needed.
This dish is usually served with sour cream.

VEAL GOULASH (Hungarian specialty)

Serves 6

2½	pounds veal stew meat (cut into one-inch cubes)
1	cup finely chopped onions
4	tablespoons vegetable oil
2–3	cups water
1	teaspoon mustard
1	lemon
3	tablespoons flour
½	cup sour cream
3	tablespoons sweet paprika
1	teaspoon salt
1	teaspoon caraway seeds

Finely chop the onions and sauté them in the hot oil until they are golden brown. Add the paprika, stir quickly, and immediately pour in a little cold water and add the meat cubes. Stir to coat the cubes with the paprika mixture; add salt and simmer for a few minutes. Add some water to cover the meat, add a teaspoon of lemon juice, and a shaving of lemon zest, the mustard and caraway seeds. Cover and simmer on medium heat until the meat is tender. (It is best to bake it in the oven) Add water as needed, but never more than to cover the meat.

Remove the meat from the sauce. Mix the sour cream with the flour, and slowly add it into the simmering sauce. Continue simmering for a few minutes on very low heat; season it and strain into a clean pot. Add the veal cubes and bring them to a boil for just a second.

Cooking Tips:
This is best served with potato dumplings or pasta.
This goulash can be prepared in advance, as it will keep fresh in the refrigerator for one week.

VEAL ROAST

Serves 6

3½	pounds boneless veal roast
5	cloves garlic
½	teaspoon black pepper
2	teaspoons salt
1	tablespoon paprika
1	tablespoon vegetable oil
½	teaspoon dry tarragon leaves
4	ripe tomatoes
½	cup water
1	bay leaf

Before serving

½ cup sour cream
1 tablespoon lemon juice

Mix all of the ingredients with the oil, and rub the mixture over entire surface of the roast. Wrap the roast in plastic, and refrigerate it overnight.

The next day, in a large, heavy skillet on high heat, brown the roast in hot oil on all sides. Transfer the meat into a large pot; add the water and the sliced tomatoes. Cover it and simmer on low heat for 1½–2 hours, or until the meat is tender. Take out the roast and slice it into half-inch portions. Strain the sauce and mix in some lemon juice and sour cream. Before serving, bring it to a quick boil.

SIDE DISHES

DOUGH FOR KNISHES (with oil)

Serves 24

2	tablespoons vegetable oil
2	tablespoons water
1	teaspoon baking powder
½	teaspoon salt
2	eggs
2	½ cups all-purpose flour
1	egg yolk mixed with 1 teaspoon of water for glazing

Combine the flour, baking powder and the salt in a bowl. Make a well in the center and add the oil, eggs and the water. With a fork or with the fingers, gradually mix the wet ingredients with the flour just enough to make a soft dough that is not sticky. On a floured board knead by hand for 5-8 minutes to an elastic and smooth dough. Place in a bowl previously coated with oil and turning the dough in it. Cover the bowl with a plastic wrap and let it rest for one hour or more. Before rolling it out, knead again for one minute. Roll it out very thin, like for a strudel, and cut out rounds of about 3 inches in diameter. Place one tablespoon of potato, kasha, or cheese filling. (See Fillings.) Fold the dough over the filling and pinch the edges to seal the knish.

Brush the tops of the dough with egg yolk and bake at 350°F for about 30 minutes, or until the top is brown. They are best served hot.

DUMPLINGS (Nockerl for goulash)

Serves 8

3	tablespoons vegetable oil
1½	tablespoons butter
1	teaspoon salt
3	tablespoons cream of wheat
2	eggs
¼	pound all-purpose flour
2	tablespoons club soda

Beat the oil, butter, eggs, and salt until they are foamy. Gradually add the flour, cream of wheat, and club soda. Beat until bubbles appear. With a teaspoon, drop the mixture bit by bit into boiling, salty water, and cook it for 3 minutes on medium heat. Drain. Melt the butter and pour it over the dumplings, stirring carefully with a wooden spoon.

KASHA WITH VARNISHKES
(Buckwheat with bow-tie noodles)

Serves 6

½	pound bow pasta
2	large onions
1	tablespoons vegetable oil
1	cup buckwheat (kasha)
1	egg
2	cups water
½	teaspoon salt
¼	teaspoon pepper

Boil the pasta in salty water until it is soft. Drain it and set aside.

To cook the buckwheat

Chop the onions and fry them in hot oil to a brownish color; remove them from the pan onto a paper towel to absorb the oil. Bring the water and salt to a boil.

Beat the egg with a fork and mix it with the buckwheat until the kernels are well coated. Heat the oil and fry the buckwheat on low heat, stirring all the time with a wooden spoon. When the buckwheat is brown and the kernels are not sticking together, pour it into the boiling water and cook over low heat until the buckwheat is soft and dry. Mix with the pasta with the buckwheat and adjust the seasoning.

Cooking Tip:
Before serving, it is good to cover the kasha dish and heat in the oven for 20 minutes.

POTATO PANCAKES (Bukovina style)

1   lb. potatoes

3   eggs

½   teaspoon salt or less

1   cup vegetable oil

      pepper to taste

Beat the eggs with the salt and pepper in a bowl.

Peel the and finely grate the potatoes by hand or in a food processor.

Squeeze out as much liquid as possible and mix with the beaten eggs.

In a large skillet, heat ½ cup oil, and drop a full tablespoon of the mixture into the hot oil.

Try not to fry more than 4-5 pancakes at a time. Flatten the pancakes a little, and lower the heat so that they cook through evenly. Let them brown on one side, turn over and brown on the other, Repeat the procedure with the rest of the oil and mixture. Pancakes should be brown and crisp at the edges. Serve immediately with sour cream on the side, or as a side dish for stews.

POTATO PANCAKES (Traditional)

Serves 10

4	large potatoes
2	large eggs
⅛	teaspoon baking powder
1	teaspoon salt
1	dash pepper
1	medium onion grated (optional)
1	tablespoon all-purpose flour
½	cup vegetable oil

Peel the potatoes and put them in ice water for one hour to prevent them from turning dark. Beat the eggs with a fork and mix them with the other ingredients. Grate the potatoes as thinly as possible, and transfer them into a sieve to drain for 8-10 minutes. Place them in a bowl, and combine with the above ingredients. Heat enough oil in a heavy skillet to a depth of about ½ ". Drop one heaped tablespoon into the bubbling oil, flattening each pancake with the back of the spoon. Cook them over medium heat until they are brown on both sides. Drain them on paper towels and serve immediately, or keep them hot in the oven.

Cooking tips:
When used during Passover, substitute the flour with matzo flour or matzo meal.
If no baking powder is used, I suggest separating the eggs and beating the whites to a peak, and then folding them into the potato mixture for a light pancake.

MAMALIGA-POLENTA (A Romanian staple)

Serves 8

1	cup yellow, medium, coarse cornmeal
½	cup cream of wheat
4	cups water
1½	tablespoon salt
2	tablespoons butter

This is not the original system of cooking mamaliga, but it works better. Pour the flour and cream of wheat into the salted cold water and bring it to a boil. Lower the heat and stir constantly for about 30 minutes. Add the butter and increase the heat. Stir well and let it rest for a few minutes. Invert it onto a serving dish. It is supposed to be cut with a thread.

Serve hot with butter, sour cream and Feta cheese, Brinza, or cottage cheese. Some people like to eat it with hot milk like a cereal.

Cooking Tips:
You can substitute one cup of water with a cup of milk.
It makes an excellent side dish for stews.

MATZAH DUMPLINGS (Kneidlach)

Serves 6

1	cup matzo meal
½	cup water
⅓	cup shortening (usually chicken fat)
1	teaspoon salt
1	dash pepper
1	tablespoon chopped parsley (optional)
4	eggs

Beat the eggs with a fork until they are foamy; add water, melted shortening, the seasonings, and mix well. Add the matzo meal, stir thoroughly, and refrigerate for one hour. With wet hands, form small balls and drop them into salted boiling water. Let it simmer covered for 20 minutes. Serve them with any stew, or just as a side dish.

MUSHROOM PIE (Lucie Sadmon)

Serves 10

4	eggs
3	cups buttermilk
½	cup vegetable oil
5	ounces feta cheese
3	cups mushrooms
3	cups self-rising flour
1	tablespoon dill weed
½	cup parmesan cheese
	salt and pepper to taste

Wash and slice the mushrooms, and sauté them in oil. Beat the eggs and mix them with the crumbled feta cheese, chopped dill weed, and all of the other ingredients. Add salt and pepper to taste. Mix well. Butter a Pyrex dish, fill it with the mixture, and top it with parmesan cheese. Bake at 350°F until the top is golden brown.

Cooking Tip: Sour cream or sour milk can be used.

NOODLE KUGEL (Aunt Tony)

Serves 12

½	pound wide egg noodles
2	eggs
1	teaspoon all-purpose flour
3½	tablespoons butter or oil
3	tablespoons grated Parmesan cheese

Cook the noodles in salty water; drain them, but do not rinse. With a fork, beat the eggs, adding the salt, pepper, and cheese. Butter a rectangular baking pan or a Pyrex and bake at 350°F for about 30 minutes. It can also be fried on the stove like an omelet.

PIROGEN
(Vareniki, Ukrainian/Jewish specialty)

Serves 8

For the dough

3	cups all-purpose flour
2	eggs
1	teaspoon salt
1	tablespoon vegetable oil
½	cup tepid water

In an electric mixer or with fingers, mix all ingredients to form an elastic dough. Knead it for a few minutes by hand on a floured surface until the dough is smooth and silky. Divide it into 3 balls, cover, and let it rest while preparing the filling.

Roll out each ball into a very thin circle or rectangle. With a glass or cookie cutter, cut out round circles and fill with any filling you desire. Seal the edges with your fingers. Fill a wide, large pot with water; add one tablespoon of salt and one tablespoon oil, and bring it to a boil. Drop the dumplings one by one; lower the heat and simmer for 10 minutes.

Prepare an oiled cookie pan. With a slotted spoon, remove the vareniki from the boiling water and place them in the cookie pan. Brush them with oil or clarified butter for serving or freezing. The ideal is to serve it straight from the pot onto a serving dish, but if that is not possible, cover the pan and heat it later in the oven. To freeze, place the pan in the freezer, and when the varenikies are completely frozen, transfer them into a plastic bag.

For the potato filling

2	pounds potatoes
2	large onions
1	tablespoon salt
1	teaspoon pepper
1	tablespoon chicken fat (optional)
4	tablespoons vegetable oil

Wash the potatoes with a brush, and boil them with the skin in salty water. Peel them and pat dry before mashing. Chop the onions and divide into 2 portions Heat 2 tablespoons of oil in a frying pan and sauté so as to obtain a brown and crisp consistency. Reserve this portion for the topping. Sauté the other portion in the remaining 2 tablespoons of oil until light brown. Mix the mashed potatoes with the fried onions and the salt and pepper to taste.

For the cheese filling

1	pound farmer cheese (or any dry cottage cheese)
1	egg yolk
1	dash sugar
	salt and pepper to taste

Mix all of the ingredients and fill the varenikies. For the cheese-filled ones, cut the dough into squares; fill and seal them to form a triangle whose ends are sealed like a tortellini.

For the meat or chicken filling

    ½   pound ground beef
    ½   pound ground pork
    1   medium onion chopped
    1   clove garlic squeezed
         milk, salt, and pepper to taste

Mix all of the ingredients, adding a little milk. Cut the dough into squares; fill and seal them to form a triangle; seal the two ends to give the form of a tortellini.

Cooking Tip:
Instead of meat, ground chicken or turkey can be used.

POTATO BALLS

Serves 12

3	pounds potatoes
2	onions
2	eggs
1	cup breadcrumbs
½	cup parmesan cheese

Peel and boil the potatoes in salty water. Drain them and puree. Finely chop the onions and sauté. Mix the potatoes with the sautéed onions, parmesan cheese, pepper, and salt. Form balls the size of large meatballs, roll them in the beaten eggs, and then in breadcrumbs. Arrange the balls on a greased cookie sheet and bake at 350°F for half an hour.

POTATO DUMPLINGS (Kartoffel Nockerl)

Serves 8

1½	pounds potatoes
¼	pound cream of wheat
2	egg yolks
½	cup all-purpose flour
	salt to taste

Boil the potatoes with the skin in salty water until they are very tender. Peel and mash them with the yolks, cream of wheat, salt, and flour to form a semi-soft dough. On a floured surface, knead the dough until it is firm, and roll it out four 2½ inch thick rolls. Cut them into small squares or rhomboids. Drop the dumplings into a large pot with salted boiling water. Lower the heat and let them simmer uncovered for 15-20 minutes. Stir them carefully so they don't stick to the bottom of the pot. With a slotted spoon, remove the dumplings onto a heated platter and sprinkle them with melted butter or margarine.

POTATO KUGEL

Serves 6

4	large potatoes
1	medium onion
2	ounces margarine or chicken fat
2	eggs
½	cup all-purpose flour
½	teaspoon baking powder
1	teaspoon salt
¼	tablespoon pepper

Peel and grate the potatoes finely, and place them in a sieve to drain for 8-10 minutes. Preheat the oven to 450°F. Pour the fat into the baking dish to melt and heat, while preparing the mixture. Whisk the eggs until they are fluffy; add the well-drained potatoes and the remaining ingredients. Adjust for salt and pepper.

Swirl the hot fat in the baking dish to coat all sides, and then pour in the potato mixture. At first, bake at 450°F for about 15 minutes, and then lower the heat to 350°F and continue baking for another hour, or until the kugel it is crisp and light brown.

POTATO OMELET (Bluma Ramler)

Serves 8

1	pound potatoes
1	tablespoon dill
1	tablespoon butter
	salt and pepper to taste

Boil the potatoes in the skin. Peel them and grind coarsely. Add dill weed, salt, and pepper. Heat the butter in a large frying pan, and when it is sizzling, pour in the potato mix and fry it on both sides like an omelet.

POTATO PUDDING (My mother's recipe)

Serves 8

8	medium potatoes
1	teaspoon cream of wheat
1	cup all-purpose flour
3	onions
4	tablespoons breadcrumbs
1	egg
	salt and pepper to taste

Boil the potatoes in salty water. Peel and mash them with the egg, cream of wheat, and salt. Mix in the flour and make a soft dough.

For the filling, chop and sauté the onions until they are light brown; add the breadcrumbs and salt and pepper to taste.

Roll out the dough on a heavily floured board to a rectangle of 13 x 9 inches. Spread the filling evenly over the dough, like in a strudel. Roll up and close the ends. Roll the strudel like a round challah. Place it in a moist kitchen towel and tie the ends with twine. Boil it in salty water for one hour. Slice it into portions and serve as a side dish with any stew.

POTATOES WITH CHEESE

Serves 8

4	large potatoes
2	medium onions
¼	pound gruyere cheese
½	cup milk
1	can cream of mushroom soup
¼	cup milk
¼	cup parmesan cheese
	salt and pepper to taste

Peel the potatoes and slice thin slices. Butter a rectangular baking dish, and cover the bottom with one layer of potato slices. Cover with thin slices of onion, grated cheese, and salt and pepper to taste. Finish with a potato layer. Dissolve the mushroom soup with the milk, and pour it on top of the potatoes. Sprinkle them with grated parmesan cheese and bake at 350°F for 30-40 minutes or until the top is brown.

POTATOES WITH ROSEMARY

Serves 4

    2   pounds red potatoes
    1   tablespoon kosher salt
    2   tablespoons rosemary
    3   tablespoons olive oil

Wash small potatoes and coat them in olive oil; sprinkle them with fresh rosemary and kosher salt. Bake them at 400°F turning them from time to time.

RATATOUILLE (Giveci)

Serves 8

2	onions
2	red peppers
4	ripe tomatoes
1	eggplant
1	cup green peas
½	pound green beans
3	carrots
1	zucchini
2	tablespoons tomato paste
3	tablespoons dill
1	tablespoon lemon juice
1	tablespoon sugar
	salt and pepper to taste

Chop and sauté the onions. Peel the ripe tomatoes, eggplant, and carrots. Cube all of the vegetables and add them to the onions. (Zucchini is optional.) Continue to sauté for a few minutes. Add the sugar, salt, pepper, lemon juice, finely chopped dill, and tomato paste.

Spoon the mixture into an 11¾ x 7½ x 1¾ inch baking dish, and bake at 350°F for 25-30 minutes. It can be served hot or cold.

ROMANIAN RISOTTO

Serves 6

1	pound white rice
1	onion
4	oz smoked bacon
1	lb potatoes
4	large tomatoes
6	green peppers
2	tablespoons parmesan
3	tablespoons butter
3	medium zucchinis
1	tablespoon sweet paprika
3	cups beef or chicken broth
	salt and pepper to taste

Sauté the rice in butter until it is light golden. Cube the peeled potatoes and sauté them with the chopped bacon and chopped onion. Cube the zucchini and tomatoes; julienne the peppers and mix it all together with the beef stock, salt, pepper, and paprika. Cover it and bake at 375°F for 20 minutes. Sprinkle it with parmesan cheese.

BREADS AND ROLLS

ROLLS FOR PASSOVER

Serves 10

⅔	cup boiling water
⅔	cup vegetable oil
1	cup matzo meal
1	teaspoon sugar
¼	teaspoon salt
4	eggs

Preheat the oven to 400°F. Bring the water, sugar, oil, and salt to a boil. Add the matzo meal, lower the flame, and stir with a wooden spoon until the edges of the pot are clear. Cool slightly and incorporate the eggs, one by one, mixing vigorously after each addition.

Divide it into 12 pieces. With greased palms, roll each one into an oblong or round ball. Lower the oven temperature to 350°F and bake for 30 minutes. Lower the temperature again to 300°F and continue baking for another 15 minutes. Total baking time is one hour. Before removing from the oven, cut one roll and test it for moisture. If the inside is still moist, bake for another few minutes. Cool on a wire rack.

Cooking Tip:
If served as cream puffs, cut into halves and fill with vanilla pudding, whipped cream, plum jam (povidla), or anything you wish; sprinkle with powdered sugar.

CHALLAH

Serves 15

1⅓	cups warm water
1½	pounds white bread flour
1	packet dry yeast or 1 ounce fresh yeast
1	tablespoon sugar
1½	teaspoons salt
3	tablespoons vegetable oil
2	large eggs

For the glaze

1	egg yolk
1	dash salt
1	teaspoon water
¼	cup poppy seeds or sesame seeds

Thoroughly mix the yeast with the dry ingredients in the large bowl of an electric mixer, and then add all of the remaining ingredients. At low speed with the kneading hook, mix the dough until a sticky ball begins to form. Increase to medium speed and knead for five minutes until the dough does not stick to the edges of the bowl. If still sticky, add one to two tablespoons of flour.

Pour the dough onto a floured wooden working board. Punch down the dough and knead out the bubbles. Knead by hand for two minutes or until it feels silky and springy. Grease a large bowl with vegetable oil; turn the dough to coat it all around. Cover with plastic wrap and let it rise in the refrigerator for nine to twenty-four hours. Should it rise too much before you are ready to bake it, just punch it down and let it rise again.

Take the risen dough from the refrigerator and let it rise at room temperature. Divide the dough in half. Cover the half you are not working on.

To braid, divide the dough into three equal parts. With your palms, roll each piece into twelve-inch strands that taper slightly at each end. Join the three strands at the upper end, stick in the point of a sharp knife into the wooden board to hold them in place, and plait the usual way. Repeat the same with the other portion.

Place the loaves on a large baking sheet, greased or lined with parchment paper. Carefully brush the braids with the egg glaze and sprinkle with poppy seeds. Let the braids rise for a second time without covering them until double in bulk.

Bake for about 30-40 minutes, or until they are shiny brown and a cake tester inserted in the center comes out dry and clean. Remove the challahs from the baking sheet and cool on wire racks. Do not slice while warm.

Twenty minutes before baking, preheat the oven to 400°F. This dough makes two loaves.

Cooking Tip:
To make a festive, round challah, make a fat rope with the dough and roll it like a snail.

KAISER ROLLS

Serves 18

4¼	cups bread flour
1	package dry yeast
1	egg
1	tablespoon butter
1	tablespoon sugar
1	teaspoon salt
1	egg white
1½	cups hot water
½	cup poppy seeds
1	teaspoon malt extract (optional)
½	cup rye flour

In a large bowl, measure and sift 3½ cups of flour together with all the dry ingredients. Mix them well and pour in the hot water and malt extract. Mix in the electric mixer with the flat beater for one minute, or until a heavy, but smooth batter forms. Add the egg, egg white, and butter. Continue beating until the batter is smooth. Remove the flat beater and continue with the dough hook. Add the remaining flour, 3-4 tablespoons at a time, until the dough is a solid, soft mass that is easily lifted from the bowl.

Place the dough on a floured work surface and knead for about one minute by hand, adding flour as needed. Brush a bowl with vegetable oil, place the dough at the bottom, and then turn it over. Cover with a plastic wrap, and let it rise for half an hour, or until it is double in bulk.

Uncover the bowl and with your fist punch down the dough. Cover it again, and let it rise for a second time until it is double in volume.

Place the dough on the floured surface and roll it into an 18"-inch-long roll. Divide into 18 pieces and shape them into smooth rounds.

Cover and let them rest for 6-7 minutes. Grease or line a baking sheet with parchment paper and sprinkle with the poppy seeds.

Flatten each roll with the palm of your hand to about three-eighths of an inch thick. Sprinkle the tops with the rye flour to prevent the cuts from running together during the baking time. With a special Kaiser roll cutter or with a sharp knife cut deep into the top of the roll so that it looks like the spokes of a wheel. Place each roll face down on the poppy seeds.

For the third rising, cover the rolls with wax paper and let them rise to less than double in size, about 35-40 minutes. Place a pan under the middle shelf. Preheat the oven to 450° F, 20 minutes before baking. A few minutes before putting the rolls into the oven, pour one cup of hot water into the pan to create a moist environment.

Take off the wax paper, turn the rolls right side up, and spray them lightly with an atomizer. Place the rolls on the middle shelf on top of the pan. Bake for 25 minutes, until brown and crispy. Three minutes after placing the rolls in the oven, spray the interior of the oven with water, away from the rolls. After fifteen minutes, turn the sheet around.

Remove the rolls, let them cool, and check if they are crusty. If not, put them back into a hot oven for another ten minutes.

MALAI (Shoshana Kesary)

Serves 12

2	eggs
1	cup yellow cornmeal
1	cup all-purpose flour
½	teaspoon baking powder
1	cup sugar
7	tablespoons melted margarine
2	tablespoons vegetable oil
1½	cups buttermilk
8	tablespoons dry cottage cheese
1	teaspoon vanilla extract
	salt to taste

Preheat the oven to 350° F. Mix all of the ingredients well, and bake them in a rectangular baking pan or in a muffin pan. Bake until they are golden brown on top.

MALAI (Romanian cornbread)

Serves 15

For the batter

1	cup all-purpose flour
1½	cups yellow, coarse cornmeal
½	cup sugar
2	teaspoons baking powder
½	tablespoon baking soda
¼	teaspoon salt
3	eggs
3	tablespoons vegetable oil
1½	cups buttermilk (sour milk is better)
6	tablespoons unsalted butter or margarine melted

For the filling

1½	cups farmer cheese
1	egg
4	tablespoons sugar
1	teaspoon salt

In a mixing bowl, stir together flour, cornmeal, sugar, baking powder, baking soda, and salt. In another bowl, whisk the eggs, oil, buttermilk, and melted butter. Stir into the flour mixture to make a smooth batter.

Combine the cheese with the egg, sugar, and salt. Mix well by hand or a food processor.

Pour half the batter into a greased 7 x 11- inch baking dish. Spread the cheese mixture evenly over the batter, then top with the remaining batter.

Bake in a preheated oven at 350°F for 40 minutes (test to see if it is done). Serve hot with sour cream or butter.

Cooking Tips:
The best cheese is farmer cheese. Ricotta is a second choice.
An optional filling as my mother used to make is: to mix the cheese with six to seven chopped scallions, one teaspoon dill, and a half teaspoon of salt; omit the sugar.

MALISNIK (Cornmeal dish)

Serves 10

4	cups buttermilk
5	eggs
1	pound farmer cheese
¾	cup yellow cornmeal
¼	cup all-purpose flour
1	teaspoon baking powder
4	tablespoons sugar
1	teaspoon salt

Mix all of the ingredients; salt and sugar to taste. (It should not be too sweet.) Bake at 350°F for about 1½ hours.

Cooking Tip:
Sour milk or yogurt can be substituted for buttermilk.

MULTIGRAIN ROLLS

1	package dry yeast
2	cups warm water
3½	cups bread flour
1	cup whole wheat flour (graham flour)
½	cup rye flour
½	cup oatmeal
¼	cup wheat gluten
2½	teaspoons salt
2	tablespoons molasses
1½	tablespoons honey
1	teaspoon bread spices (See Tips)

In a deep bowl, sprinkle the yeast over the warm water (about 110°F), and let it stand until bubbles appear. In the large bowl of an electric mixer, combine the flour with all the dry ingredients, spices included. Add the honey, molasses, and yeast mixture. With the kneading hook, knead on medium speed for 10 minutes or until the dough is soft and smooth. On a lightly floured working surface, knead by hand for one minute and shape into a ball. Place the ball into a lightly oiled bowl and turn it with the oiled side up. Cover with a plastic wrap and let it rise in a warm place, away from drafts, until doubled.

Preheat the oven to 400°F. Before putting in the rolls to bake, spray the interior of the oven with cold water or throw in a few ice cubes to create a moist environment.

Punch down the raised dough with your fist, place it onto your working surface, and knead by hand for another few minutes. Form a roll and cut it into 2–2½- inch portions. Knead each piece for a few seconds to form a round roll. Sprinkle with oatmeal and bake for thirty to forty minutes.

POTATO BREAD (Totch; Bukovina specialty)

Serves 20

2	pounds Idaho potatoes
1½	packet dry yeast
¼	cup warm water
¼	teaspoon sugar
4	tablespoons vegetable oil
¼	teaspoon pepper
1	tablespoon salt
1	onion (optional)
2	eggs

2½-3 cups all-purpose flour

Dissolve the yeast in the warm water, adding the sugar and topping with two tablespoons flour. Peel and grate potatoes in a food processor on the fine grater blade (like carrots). Pour out a little bit of the liquid, but not all of it. Add the eggs, oil, salt, pepper, yeast mixture, and one cup of flour. If onion is used, grate it finely and add to the mixture. Mix well and cover the top with two cups flour. Cover the mixture with a towel or plastic sheet, and let it rise until the top of the flour cracks. Mix again and add more flour if needed to obtain a thick mass, but not too thick.

Butter or oil a 9 x 13" baking dish, pour in the mixture, cover, and let it rise again for another 20 minutes. Preheat the oven to 250°F. Bake first at 250°F for 10 minutes. Raise temperature to 375°F–400°F for 1-2 hours. After the first 45 minutes, brush the top with oil and bake until brown.

WHOLE WHEAT BREAD

Serves 12

2½   cups whole wheat flour (graham flour)
2½   cups bread flour, or unbleached flour
¼   cup molasses
½   cup nonfat dry milk
1   tablespoon salt
2   packets dry yeast
3   tablespoons shortening at room temperature
½   teaspoon caramel extract (optional)
2   cups hot water (120°F–130°F)

Dissolve the yeast in a ¼ cup of warm water. Let it stand for 10 minutes until bubbles form.

Sift all of the dry ingredients; add the dissolved yeast, dry milk, molasses, water, and shortening. In an electric mixer with the flat beater, mix all ingredients for a few minutes. With the dough hook, continue kneading for 20 minutes on medium speed. When the sides of the bowl are clean, turn dough on a floured surface and knead by hand for another 5 minutes. Oil a large bowl, place the round side down, and then turn it over and cover with plastic wrap to rise in warm environment until it is double. Push it down with a fist to push out all the air. Divide it into two portions, or make rolls. Put the dough in greased baking forms and let it rise again until double.

Preheat oven to 350°F. Before putting in the bread, throw in a full cup of ice cubes. Bake until a hollow sound is produced when tapping the bread.

WHOLE WHEAT ROLLS

Serves 12

¼	cup warm water
2	packages dry yeast
1	cup milk
1½	tablespoons unsalted butter
2½	tablespoons granulated sugar
1½	teaspoons salt
1½	cups whole wheat flour (graham flour)
1½	cups all-purpose flour
2	tablespoons melted, unsalted butter
¼	cup warm water (110°F)

Dissolve the yeast in a quarter cup of warm water and let it rest for 8-10 minutes, until it starts rising. Bring the milk to a boil; remove from the heat. Mix in the butter, sugar, and salt; stir until melted. Set it aside to cool until lukewarm.

In a large bowl of the electric mixer, combine the yeast mixture, milk, whole wheat, and all-purpose flour; mix on medium speed until the dough has pulled together.

Turn out the dough onto a lightly floured surface and knead by hand for 10 minutes, until it is smooth and elastic. Lightly oil a deep bowl, place the dough in it, and turn it to coat all sides with the oil. Cover with plastic wrap or a damp kitchen towel, and let it rise in a warm place away from drafts until it doubles in volume.

Deflate the risen dough and turn it on a lightly floured working surface. Cut the dough into 12 portions and shape each piece into an oval. Grease or line with parchment papers, a large baking sheet, or two small baking sheets. Place the rolls an inch apart, and brush the top with melted butter. Cover again and let them rise until double in volume. Preheat the oven to 375°F, and bake the rolls until golden brown, about 15-20 minutes.

DESSERTS

APPLE STRUDEL

Serves 12

Makes 4 strudels

2	pounds tart apples
20	sheets filo dough
8	ounces unsalted butter, melted
1	lemon
¾	cup walnuts, coarsely chopped
¼	cup raisins (preferably golden)
1	teaspoon cinnamon
½	cup very fine breadcrumbs, or ground leftover cookies, or ground almonds
¾	cup sugar
1	teaspoon vanilla extract
4	tablespoons confectioners' sugar

Make four strudel rolls. Peel and core the apples. Squeeze lemon juice into a bowl, and coat the apples in the juice to prevent them from turning brown. Cut into quarter-inch pieces or slices and combine the apples with all of the other ingredients.

Handle filo dough according to the instructions. Lay two sheets on a work surface and brush the top one lightly with melted butter. Brush four more sheets with butter, to a total of five sheets.

Divide the filling into four parts. Spread a quarter of the breadcrumbs on the entire last sheet. Spread a quarter of the filling on top of the crumbs, leaving a one-inch border on all sides. Starting from the long side, very tightly roll up the strudel, tucking in the sides halfway so that the filling does not fall out. Carefully transfer the rolls onto a greased baking sheet, seam side down. Brush the tops with more melted butter and bake them in a preheated oven at 350°F for thirty-five to forty minutes, until golden and crisp. Sprinkle with confectioners' sugar, cut into portions, and serve them warm or cold.

Cooking Tip:
The same filo procedure can be filled with sour cherries or farmer cheese.

CHEESE PALATSCHINKEN (Sweet Cheese Crepes)

Serves 12

1	cup all-purpose flour
1¼	cups milk
⅔	cup water
¼	tablespoon oil
1	egg
½	teaspoon salt
1-2	tablespoons oil for frying

For the filling

1	pound farmer cheese
½	pound cream cheese
½	cup sugar
1½	lemon for zest
3	egg yolks
1	teaspoon vanilla extract
¼	cup raisins (or currants)
2	tablespoons strawberry jam

For the topping

½	cup confectioners' sugar
1	cup sour cream
	cinnamon

Add the milk and water to the flour gradually, beating vigorously. Add the egg, salt, and oil, and beat the batter until it is smooth. Leave it to rest for one to two hours.

Heat a nonstick frying pan or a special one for crepes with a bottom no wider than 8 inches, and grease it very slightly with oil. Pour less than half a cup of the batter into the pan, and move the pan around until its entire surface is covered with batter. The pancakes should be thin. As soon as the pancake is slightly browned and detached at the edges, turn it over with a spatula and cook only a moment on the other side. Continue until all the batter is used and put the pancakes in a pile. Remember to mix the batter from time to time.

Soak the raisins in a little rum for half an hour, then pat them dry with a paper towel.

Blend the farmer cheese and the cream cheese with the sugar, egg yolks, lemon zest, vanilla, and jam in the food processor, or with a fork.

Take one pancake at the time, and put two heaping tablespoons of filling on the bottom half; fold the edges over the filling, tuck in the sides to trap the filling, and roll it up into a slim roll. Place the rolls side by side in a greased oven dish. Sprinkle with butter and bake in a preheated over at 375°F for 20 minutes. Serve hot, dusted with confectioners' sugar and cinnamon, and pass the sour cream for people to help themselves. They can also be served with blueberry or strawberry preserves.

Cooking Tips:
For apple filling: Peel and core two pounds of apples. Steam them in a pan with the lid on and with only a drop of water. Puree and sweeten with sugar to taste; add one teaspoon of cinnamon and a few gratings of nutmeg.

For cherry filling: Pit two pounds of cherries and steam them in a pan with the lid on. Add sugar to taste. The cherries can be mixed with half a cup of ground almonds or two to three drops of almond extract.

BREAD PUDDING WITH CARAMEL SAUCE

Serves 12

7	cups white bread (fresh or stale)
½	cup golden raisins
½	cup unsalted butter
4	eggs
1	cup granulated sugar
¼	cup light brown sugar
1	teaspoon nutmeg
2	teaspoons vanilla extract
2	cups milk
2	cups half-and-half

Caramel sauce:

½	cup unsalted butter
1	cup packed light brown sugar
¼	teaspoon salt
1	teaspoon vanilla extract
½	cup evaporated milk

Remove crusts from bread. Cube bread and place into a greased 9 x 13 inch baking dish. Sprinkle raisins over the bread and drizzle with melted butter, but do not mix. Set this aside.

In a large mixing bowl, beat the eggs until they are broken up; blend in the sugars, nutmeg, and vanilla. Add half-and-half and the milk, but do not overbeat; bubbles are not necessary. Pour the milk mixture over the bread cubes and let them soak for 15 minutes, gently patting the bread into the milk mixture. Sprinkle with nutmeg.

Preheat the oven to 350°F and bake for 55 minutes, checking after 40 minutes to make sure the top is not too brown. Should it be too brown, cover it lightly with foil and bake 15 minutes longer until the pudding is puffy and golden brown. Remove onto a rack and let it cool.

Caramel sauce:
In a small saucepan over medium heat, melt the butter and brown sugar, whisking vigorously as the mixture cooks. Bring to a boil, remove from heat, and whisk in the salt, vanilla, and evaporated milk. The sauce can be made ahead and reheated in the microwave.

Cut the cooled pudding into squares and top each serving with the hot caramel sauce.

CHOCOLATE RUM BALLS

Serves 20

1	small ready-made chocolate cake with chocolate filling and frosting
2	tablespoons cognac
1	cup walnuts
1	cup heavy whipping cream
2	teaspoons powdered sugar
2	tablespoons cherry liqueur
6	ounces semi-sweet chocolate
½	cup chocolate sprinkles (decor)

Melt the chocolate and let it cool. Grind the cake in a food processor. Add the melted chocolate and the remaining ingredients, except the sprinkles. Mix it well and refrigerate overnight.

Wet your hands with cold water and form small balls. Roll them in the chocolate sprinkles and freeze them. Keep frozen until serving, as they thaw very fast.

COLD RICE DESSERT

Serves 6

1	cup white rice
2½	cups milk
1	teaspoon vanilla extract
4	tablespoons sugar
1	dash salt

For the topping

½ cup sour cream
1 teaspoon vanilla extract
½ cup sugar
½ cup fruit preserves (optional)

Cook the rice in milk with the salt for 20 minutes, covered. At the end, add the sugar and vanilla. Wet the forms of dessert bowls or cups with cold water, fill with the rice, and let them cool. Before serving, invert the forms onto serving plates like gelatin. Top them with sour cream, vanilla, and sugar, or with any fruit preserves you like.

CREAM PUFFS

Serves 12

For the dough

1	cup water
½	cup butter
¼	teaspoon salt
1	cup sifted all-purpose flour
4	eggs
1	pinch salt

For the filling

1	packet vanilla pudding
1	cup milk
½	cup whipped cream
½	teaspoon vanilla extract

For topping

¾	cup powdered sugar

Preheat the oven at 400°F. In a saucepan, bring water, butter, and salt to full rolling boil. Remove the pan from the heat and quickly stir in the flour, mixing vigorously with a wooden spoon until the mixture leaves the sides of the pan in a ball. If necessary, replace briefly over low heat. Place the mixture in the bowl of an electric mixer with a wire beater. On medium speed, add the eggs, one at the time, beating approximately 30 seconds after each addition. Scrape the bowl occasionally. After adding the final egg, increase the speed, and beat for 15 seconds.

Drop rounded tablespoons of dough onto a greased cookie sheet, forming mounds that are 3 inches apart, and shaping them high. This can also be done with a cookie press or a pastry tube, using the largest size.

Bake at 400°F for 10 minutes. Lower the heat to 350°F and bake for 25 minutes, or until the puffs have doubled in size. Remove it from the oven and cut a small slit into the side of each. Let them stand for 10 minutes in a turned-off oven with the door ajar. Take them out and cool completely; cut off the tops and fill with the custard; cover and sprinkle with powdered sugar.

Prepare pudding according to the instructions, but use only one cup of milk. Add vanilla extract. Whip the cream with two teaspoons of powdered sugar. Carefully mix the cooled pudding with the whipped cream. Fill the puffs, cover, and sprinkle with powdered sugar.

For appetizers
Split puffs and fill them with chicken, ham, tuna, or egg salad.

DIPLOMATIC PUDDING

Serves 20

5	egg yolks
1	cup sugar
1	cup milk
2	cans fruit cocktail in heavy syrup
4	cups heavy whipping cream
1	tablespoon rum
1	teaspoon vanilla or almond extract
4	packets unflavored gelatin
4	tablespoons cold water
10	tablespoons powdered sugar

Strain the fruit and save the juice of only one can. In a double boiler, mix the egg yolks, sugar, and milk; stir constantly until the mixture gets thick.

Dissolve the gelatin in the cold water. Bring the juice to a boil, add the dissolved gelatin and bring that to another boil. Add the other ingredients, except the cream. Cool. Whip the cream with the powdered sugar. Take out one cup for icing. Fold the remaining whipped cream into the cold pudding. Refrigerate it overnight. Decorate with the leftover whipping cream, and then decorate with maraschino cherries or anything to your liking.

APRICOT OR PLUM DUMPLINGS

Serves 12

For the dough

1	cup all-purpose flour
1	cup water
1	dash salt
4	tablespoons unsalted butter

For the filling

12	apricots
12	sugar lumps

When using fresh apricots or plums, pit and blot out moisture with a paper towel. Replace the pit with a sugar lump. When using dry apricots, soak them overnight in water. The next day, blot the moisture with a paper towel and place a sugar lump inside.

For the topping

½	cup fine breadcrumbs
12	tablespoons unsalted butter
½	cup sugar
1	teaspoon cinnamon
¼	cup ground walnuts
½	cup sour cream (optional)

Bring water, salt, and butter to a boil. Stir in the flour at once, and mix vigorously. Remove from heat and continue mixing until the sides of pot are clean. Cool the dough and roll out on a floured board. With a glass or larger cookie cutter, cut out circles to about ¾" thick, or just tear pieces; fill with the fruit and close to form a ball. Drop them into boiling water, lower heat, and simmer for 15 minutes, slightly turning the dumplings. While still simmering, remove the balls with a slotted spoon and drizzle them with melted butter.

In a skillet, melt the butter and fry fine breadcrumbs until they are brown. Mix them with ground walnuts, sugar, and cinnamon. Sprinkle crumbs on top of the dumplings and serve hot. They can also be served with just sugar, cinnamon, or sour cream. They can be frozen.

FARMER CHEESE DUMPLINGS

Serves 8

1	pound farmer cheese
4	Kaiser rolls (or 4 slices of white bread without the crust)
1	cup cream of wheat
2	eggs
1	dash salt
1	dash sugar
1	cup milk

Topping

1 cup breadcrumbs
4 tablespoons unsalted butter
½ cup sugar
1 teaspoon cinnamon (optional)
½ cup sour cream (optional)

Peel Kaiser rolls and cut into small cubes. Soak them in milk and squeeze dry. Press the cheese and soaked bread through a strainer. Beat the eggs slightly and mix them with the other ingredients. Let the mixture rest for one hour.

Bring slightly salted water to a boil. With wet hands, form small balls and drop them into the boiling water. Lower the heat and let them simmer slowly for 15 minutes.

Separately, fry the breadcrumbs in butter until they are brown. Roll the cheese balls in the crumbs; sprinkle them with sugar and cinnamon They can also be served with stewed prunes or other compotes; I like it with sour cream, sugar, and cinnamon.

FRUIT COMPOTE (Ruth's version)

Serves 8

½	cup dried prunes
½	cup dried apricots
1	cup fresh apples sliced
1	cup fresh pears sliced
1	cinnamon stick
½	small lemon or a ¼ of a large one
1	cup sugar (substitute with artificial sweetener)

Place the dried fruits in a large pot with plenty of water, and bring them to a boil. Add the sugar, cinnamon stick, and lemon. (If a sugar substitute will be used, add it only at the very end or the compote will taste bitter.) Lower the heat and let it simmer until the apricots are half done. Now add the fresh fruit and continue simmering until they are tender. Taste for sweetness. Cool it and refrigerate. Serve cold.

RAW CAROTS DESSERT (Gezer chai; an Israeli specialty)

Serves 4

6	medium carrots
½	cup orange juice
¼	cup raisins
2	teaspoons lemon juice
	sugar or sugar substitute to taste

In a food processor, grate the carrots on the fine grater. In a deep bowl, mix the grated carrots with all of the other ingredients. Adjust for sweetness and serve cold.

PARFAIT (Lucie Sadmon)

Serves 8

2	cups whipped cream
2	packets instant vanilla pudding
1	cup milk
12	ounces meringues
4	ounces pecans (or walnuts)
1	tablespoon instant coffee

Crush the meringues and the pecans. Prepare instant vanilla pudding with <u>one</u> cup of milk. Beat whipping cream to a stiff peak. Carefully incorporate the whipping cream into the pudding, add the meringues, the pecans, and the coffee mix them all together and freeze. Serve it like ice cream.

Cooking Tip:
Any kind of nuts can be used.

PLOMBIER (Russian ice cream)

Serves 12

2	cups heavy whipping cream
5	egg whites
1	(15¼ ounces) can fruit cocktail in heavy syrup
6	dried prunes
6	dried apricots
½	cup raisins
½	cup walnuts (or almonds)
½	cup maraschino cherries
1	teaspoon almond extract
½	cup powdered sugar
12	maraschino cherries for serving

Drain the fruit cocktail. Cut up all of the dried fruits and chop the walnuts. Whip the cream with powdered sugar. Beat the egg whites until they are stiff, but not dry. Carefully mix all of the above ingredients and freeze in a rectangular Pyrex, or a lasagna baking dish. Before serving, leave the mixture for a few minutes at room temperature. Cut squares, put a maraschino cherry in the center of each portion, and serve them like ice cream.

POTATO PLUM DUMPLINGS

Serves 8

For the dough

1	pound potatoes, mealy, high starch
2	eggs
2	tablespoons cream of wheat
1	dash salt
1¼–1½	cups all-purpose flour

For the filling

8	very ripe Italian plums
8	lumps sugar

For the topping

1	cup fine breadcrumbs
½	cup sugar
½	cup unsalted butter
	cinnamon (optional)

Wash and cook the potatoes in their skin; peel and mash while they are still hot. (I like to mash them with a fork to feel small potato parts in the dough.) Cover them and refrigerate overnight. The next day, add the eggs, salt, the cream of wheat and flour at once, and knead quickly. Add flour if necessary, depending on the moisture in the potatoes. Do not knead too much, as that may cause the dumplings to open.

Wash the plums and open them just enough to take out the pit. Dry the outside and inside of the plum with a paper towel. Replace the pit with a sugar lump.

On a floured board, form either a ball or a long roll, and let it rest covered at room temperature for about one hour. If you made a ball, roll it out to a thickness of about ½"; cut out round or square shapes and place a plum in the center. If you made a roll, cut it into eight portions, flatten each one with your hands, and proceed as above. With your palms, form a ball, squeezing and pressing the dumpling to get out any air trapped inside. Make sure dumplings are well sealed. Place them on a floured surface until they are ready to be dropped into the boiling water.

Melt the butter in a large pan, add the breadcrumbs, and fry them on low heat until they are golden brown. Remove them from stove and add the sugar. Cinnamon is optional.

In a wide pot that will allow all eight dumplings to fit at the bottom, bring slightly salted water to a boil. Drop the dumplings in at once, lower the heat, and let them simmer for ten minutes. Remove dumplings with a slotted spoon onto a heated platter; top them with the crumbs mixture and serve.

Cooking Tip:
If Italian plums are not available, and the ones you find are very big, cut them in half.
The same dough is good for any fruit filling, like apricots and strawberries, as well as for small dumplings for meat stews.

NUSSKIPFERL (Nut crescents)

Serves 24

For the dough

4	ounces unsalted butter
4	ounces cream cheese
½	cup sour cream
1	pinch salt
1¼	cup all-purpose flour
1	egg yolk

Filling

¼ cup powdered sugar
2 teaspoons ground cinnamon
4 tablespoons raisins
¼ cup finely chopped walnuts

In an electric food processor or mixer, beat the cold butter to a cream. Add the cream cheese, sour cream, and salt, and blend well. Add the flour until the dough holds together in a soft ball. Adjust by either adding another tablespoon of sour cream or more flour. Wrap in a plastic wrap and refrigerate for minimum 4 hours.

Divide the dough into four. With floured hands, roll each piece into a ball. On a floured board and using a floured rolling pin, roll each ball out into a large, round, and thin circle, dusting it each time you roll it over. With a pointed knife, cut each round into six triangular wedges (like a torte). Sprinkle each wedge evenly with the filling mixture. Roll up each triangle tightly with the filling inside, beginning from the wider, curved end, and finishing with the point in the middle. Curve the rolls slightly into little crescents and place them, point side down, on well-greased baking trays, leaving enough space for them to rise.

Brush with egg yolk and bake in a preheated oven 350°F for 20-25 minutes, or until they are slightly colored. Let them cool.

STUFFED BAKED APPLES

Serves 6

6	large baking apples
1	cup roasted almonds or hazelnuts
½	cup heavy whipping cream
½	cup golden raisins
¼	cup cognac
½	cup honey
½	cup dark rum, or water plus rum extract
1	cup whipped cream
3	teaspoons confectioners' sugar for the whipping cream

I like to bake the apples in the microwave for about 10-15 minutes. For a conventional oven, preheat to 400°F. Cut the tops of apples and put them aside. Core but don't peel the apples. Chop the almonds and the raisins. Soak the raisins in the cognac. In a bowl, combine the nuts, cream, and soaked raisins. Fill the apples with this mixture and cover them with the cut-off tops. In a deep baking dish, arrange the apples side by side. Separately, mix the honey with the rum and pour it over the apples. Bake them for thirty-five to forty minutes. Baste them with the sauce every ten minutes.

Whip the cream, adding the confectioners' sugar. Serve the apples hot with the whipped cream on the side, or serve them chilled with the whipped cream on top.

SWEET NOODLE KUGEL (Lokshen Kugel)

Serves 12

½	pound wide egg noodles
4	tart apples
3	eggs
½	pound cottage cheese
¼	cup raisins, black or golden
⅔	cup sugar
¼	cup walnuts or almonds
1	teaspoon lemon zest
½	lemon juice
½	pint sour cream
1	teaspoon cinnamon (optional)
½	cup milk

Boil the noodles in slightly salty water until they are almost done. Drain them well. Peel, core, and grate or coarsely chop the apples, and mix them with the lemon juice and zest. Add the cottage cheese, sour cream, and milk, and mix the remaining ingredients together well. Pour the mixture into a rectangular Pyrex, or similar baking pan, lined with parchment paper or just greased. Cover it with foil and bake in a preheated over at 350°F for about 50 minutes, or until the kugel is lightly browned on top. Take off the foil if it is not brown enough.

Cooking Tip:
Orange zest can be used instead of lemon.

FILLINGS

APPLE PIE FILLING

Serves 10

8	apples (tart)
1	tablespoon all-purpose flour
¾	cup sugar
½	teaspoon cinnamon
1	tablespoon lemon juice

Peel and grate or slice apples. Mix all of the ingredients and fill the pie. Bake at 450°F for 25 minutes or at 325°F for 40 minutes.

Cooking Tip:
Use tart apples.

FILLING FOR RUGELACH OR NUT CRESCENTS

½   cup heavy whipping cream
1¼   cups ground walnuts
¾   cup sugar
1   tablespoon rum
1   tablespoon lemon zest
¼   cup raisins

In a small pot, mix all of the ingredients, and bring them to a quick boil. Remove the pot from stove, and let it cool. With this mixture you can fill any kind of pastries.

FILLING FOR SWEET CHEESE STRUDEL

1	cup farmer cheese
1	slice white bread
¼	cup milk
2	eggs
1	teaspoon vanilla extract
2	teaspoons lemon zest
½	cup raisins
½	cup sugar
½	cup raspberries preserve (optional)

Cut off the crust and sprinkle the bread slice with the milk. Press out the milk and press the soaked bread with the cheese through a sieve. Beat the eggs slightly and mix all the ingredients well. Fill any strudel dough.

POPPY SEED FILLING

1	cup poppy seeds
¼	cup milk
2	tablespoons honey
4	tablespoons sugar
4	tablespoons raisins
1	tablespoon lemon juice
1½	tablespoons unsalted butter
1	teaspoon lemon zest

Put poppy seeds in a pot and simmer in the milk, stirring constantly for 15 minutes or until it is thick. Add honey, sugar, and raisins, and cook for five minutes more. Add the lemon zest, lemon juice, and butter; mix well. Let it cool.

Cooking Tip:
This filling serves for many recipes requiring poppy seeds.

MOCHA CREAM FILLING

4	egg yolks
2	tablespoons instant coffee
1	tablespoon sugar
¼	cup water
1	tablespoon cornstarch
1	teaspoon unsalted butte
¾	tablespoon flour

In a double boiler mix all ingredients, except the butter. Bring to a boil, lower heat and mix until slightly thickened. Let the cream cool and beat in the butter.

MUSHROOM FILLING

10½ ounces mushrooms
2   medium onions
1   red pepper
1   egg
1   cup breadcrumbs
1   egg yolk

Slice the onions, julienne the pepper, and chop the mushrooms. Sauté the onions first, then the pepper, and lastly, the well dried mushrooms. Let it cool; add one egg, pepper, salt, and dill. Roll out the dough, spread crumbs about 3 inches away from the border, top with filling, and roll into a strudel. Glaze with one egg yolk and bake in a preheated oven at 350°F until the top is brown.

WALNUT FILLING

2	cups ground walnuts
½	cup sugar
½	cup apricot preserves
½	cup heavy cream
¼	cup dark rum
½	cup raisins

In a saucepan, combine the walnuts, sugar, apricot preserves, and cream; cook for 5 minutes, stirring constantly. Combine the rum and raisins. Let them stand for 10 minutes, and then add them to the nut mixture. Cool completely.

SOUR CHERRY FILLING:

1	can well-drained sour pitted cherries or
	(1 pound pitted sweet fresh cherries)
½	cup sugar
½	chopped walnuts
¼	cup unseasoned bread crumbs

Combine all ingredients and fill any strudel dough.

KASHA FILLING FOR KNISHES
(Buckwheat)

2	large onions
1	tablespoons vegetable oil
1	cup buckwheat (kasha)
1	egg
2	cups water
½	teaspoon salt
¼	teaspoon pepper

Chop the onions and fry them in hot oil to a brownish color; remove them from the pan onto a paper towel to absorb the oil. Bring the water and salt to a boil.

Beat the egg with a fork and mix until the buckwheat kernels are well coated. Heat the oil and fry the buckwheat on low heat, stirring all the time with a wooden spoon. When the buckwheat is brown and the kernels are not sticking together, pour it into the boiling water and cook over low heat until the buckwheat is soft and dry. Adjust seasoning.

POTATO FILLING FOR KNISHES

1	pound potatoes
3	tablespoons vegetable oil or chicken fat
2	medium chopped onions
	salt and pepper to taste

Fry the onions in the fat until they are golden brown. Boil the potatoes with the skin in salty water; cool, peel, and mash them. Mix in the fried onions, pepper, and salt.

CAKES

ALMOND-DATES TORTE (Bluma Ramler)

For the dough

5	egg whites
¾	cup almonds unpeeled, ground
10	tablespoons pitted and thinly sliced dates
1	tablespoon flour for coating the dates
1	tablespoon flour for the mixture
1	tablespoon corn starch
¾	cup powdered sugar
1	tablespoon orange zest

For the filling

5	egg yolks
6	tablespoons powdered sugar
4½	ounces semi-sweet chocolate
3	tablespoons strong coffee
1	cup hot milk
1¼	tablespoons unflavored gelatin
2	tablespoons hot water
¾	cup heavy whipping cream

Beat the egg whites to a firm peak, gradually adding the powdered sugar. In a bowl, mix the almonds, dates coated in flour, and orange zest. Carefully and slowly incorporate the mixture with a spatula into the egg whites.

Butter and flour a nine-inch spring form pan. Fill with the mixture and bake for 15 minutes at 400°F until done or when tester comes out dry. Remove from oven and leave in the pan.

Melt the chocolate with the coffee and hot milk in a double boiler. In a small pan, on very low heat, whisk the egg yolks with the sugar, adding the chocolate mixture and stirring all of the time. Dissolve the gelatin in the two tablespoons of hot water and whisk it into the cream. Remove it from stove and let it cool. Whip the heavy cream and fold into the chocolate mixture. Pour over the baked cake in its mold and refrigerate for at least two hours before serving.

ALMOND TORTE

Serves 15

6	egg whites
6	tablespoons sugar
1	cup almonds
1	tablespoon all-purpose flour
1	tablespoon corn starch

Peel and lightly toast the almonds. Grind them finely. Beat the egg whites, gradually adding the sugar until firm but not dry. Carefully incorporate the almonds and the flours. Preheat oven to 325° F and bake until tops are light brown. Bake 3 round layers in a 9" spring-form pans, and fill and frost with mocha cream. The same mixture can be baked in a 10½ x 15 ½ x 1 inch jelly roll pan, lined with parchment paper. While baking in the jelly roll pan wet and firmly wring out a smooth kitchen towel and spread it out on a flat surface. Remove cake from the oven and cool on a wire rack. Cut around the edges, and invert it onto the damp towel. Remove pan, peel off the parchment paper, and roll with the towel like a strudel. Roll firmly, but don't squash the cake. When the cake is completely cooled, unroll it and fill with the same mocha cream. (Leave some for the icing.) With the same damp towel, roll the filled pastry and remove the towel. Decorate with the remaining cream.

For the filling: see Mocha Cream Frosting

APPLE BREAD PUDDING

8	French rolls
1	cup milk
2	tablespoons sugar
3	eggs
2	lbs. tart apples
1	teaspoon lemon zest
3	teaspoons lemon juice
½	teaspoon cinnamon
⅓	cup raisins
4	oz. unsalted butter melted
¼	cup sugar

For the meringue

3	egg whites
⅓	cup sugar
1	dash salt
¼	cup crushes walnuts
¼	cup sugar

Cut off crusts and slice the rolls. Mix the eggs with the 2 tablespoons sugar and the milk. Dip the roll slices in the milk mixture until they are well soaked.

Peel and thinly slice the apples and mix them with the ¼ cup sugar, cinnamon, lemon zest, juice, raisins and the melted butter.

In a 9" greased spring-form pan or a rectangular baking dish, arrange layers of bread alternating with apple mixture, ending with a bread layer. Press the last layer firmly into the mold and cover the top with a greased wax paper. Bake at 350º F for one hour.

The meringue

In a small bowl of an electric mixer, beat the egg whites with the salt at medium speed until soft peaks form. Increase to high speed and add 2 tablespoons sugar at the time. Beat until sugar is completely dissolved and whites stand in peaks.

After one hour, remove the cake from the oven; peel off the wax paper and quickly spread the meringue evenly on top. Sprinkle with sugar and walnuts, and bake for another 10-15 minutes, or until meringue is light brown.

Can be served hot or cold.

APPLE/FRUIT CAKE (Lucie Sadmon)

Serves 10

2	pounds apples (or other fruits)
4	ounces unsalted butter
½	cup sugar
2	eggs
1	cup all-purpose flour
2	tablespoons cornstarch
2	teaspoons baking powder
4	tablespoons milk
1	teaspoon vanilla extract
1	lemon

For the streusel topping

½	cup flour
½	cup sugar
6	ounces butter (or margarine)
¼	teaspoon cinnamon

Using fingers, crumble the butter, flour, sugar, and cinnamon, and sprinkle them on top of the fruit. Bake at 350°F for about one hour or until streusel is brown. (Optional: sprinkle powdered sugar on top of streusel.). Cool before serving.

Preheat oven to 350º F. Peel, core, and slice the apples and place them in a bowl with ice water and lemon juice (this prevents them from turning brown), then drain.

In an electric mixer at medium speed, beat the butter, sugar, and eggs to a pale color. Sift the dry ingredients, and add them gradually to the butter mixture at low speed. Alternate the addition of flour with the milk. Grease and flour a 9" spring form pan or a rectangular baking dish. Spread the dough at the bottom; top with the thinly sliced apples and sprinkle with the streusel. If using a rectangular dish, arrange fruit in rows; sprinkle with the streusel.

Cooking tip: You can use any fruit in season or a mixture of various fruits.

APPLE TORTE (Lucie Sadmon)

Serves 10-14

For the dough

8	ounces unsalted butter
½	cup sugar
3	egg yolks
2	cups all-purpose flour
2	teaspoons baking powder

For the filling

2	pounds tart apples
¼	cup raisins
½	cup walnuts
½	teaspoon cinnamon
¼	cup sugar
1	teaspoon lemon zest

For the top

3	egg whites
½	cup sugar

Mix the flour, yolks, and sugar in an electric mixer, or with a fork or fingers. Divide the dough into two parts. Line the bottom and rims of a 9" spring form pan, previously buttered and sprinkled with flour.

Peel, slice or grate the apples. Mix with the remaining ingredients and fill the form. Roll out the other half of the dough to the size of the spring form pan on wax paper. Cover the apple mixture and leave the paper on. Bake at 350°F at first for 15 minutes. Lower the heat to 300°F and continue baking for another 30 minutes.

Beat egg whites with the ½ cup sugar to make a meringue. Remove the paper, spread the meringue over the cake, and bake for another 30 minutes, or until the meringue is brown. Cool away from drafts.

APRICOT PIE

Serves 12

2	egg yolks
1½	cups all-purpose flour
6	ounces unsalted butter
¼	cup sugar
1	teaspoon baking powder
1	dash salt
1	teaspoon lemon juice
2	pounds pitted apricots

For the meringue

3	egg whites
¼	teaspoon lemon juice
⅔	cup powdered sugar

Mix all of the ingredients into a soft dough and roll out a circle to fit into a pie form or any other baking dish. Bake at 350°F until it is half way done. Remove from the oven and top with the halved apricots. Continue baking for twenty minutes. Beat the egg whites with the lemon juice and sugar to a stiff meringue. Spread it evenly over the apricots and bake until brown.

Cooking Tip:
The same recipe is good for any fruit in season.

BAKLAVA (The pastry of the rich)

This multi-layered, nut-filled pastry has been known as a Romanian/Jewish dessert made for special festivities. It is of Turkish/Greek origin, but it must have been adopted by the Romanians during the rule of the Ottoman Empire.

Serves 30

1	pound filo pastry sheets
3½	cups chopped pistachios, almonds, walnuts, or hazelnuts
6	ounces melted unsalted butter
½	cup sunflower oil or vegetable oil
4	tablespoons sugar
1	teaspoon cinnamon
1	dash ground clove
1	teaspoon lemon zest

For the syrup

1	cup water
2	cups sugar
1	teaspoon lemon juice
2	tablespoons orange blossom water or rose water
3	cloves
1	stick cinnamon
½	cup honey
1	teaspoon orange zest

Buy the finest filo sheets you can get. Grease a rectangular baking pan (13 x 9 x 2). Place half of the pastry sheets at the bottom, brushing every other sheet evenly with a butter and oil mixture, easing the sheets into the corners, folding and overlapping as necessary. Trim the edges that spill over the rim. Combine the nuts, sugar, cinnamon, lemon zest and clove, and spread evenly over the sheets. Repeat the process with the remaining sheets, brushing each, including the top with the butter/oil mixture.

Preheat the oven to 350°F. With a sharp, pointed knife, cut the baklava into diamond-shaped pieces of about two to three inches long and 1½–2 inches wide. Bake for one hour. If top is not browned, raise the temperature to 400°F for a few minutes. While the pastry is in the oven, prepare the syrup.

In a saucepan, combine the water, sugar, honey, lemon juice, orange zest, cinnamon stick, and cloves. Simmer for ten to fifteen minutes, and then add the orange blossom water. Let it cool. Discard the cinnamon stick. Take the baklava out of the oven, cool for 5 minutes, and pour the syrup over it.

Cooking Tip:
In Turkey, rose water is used. I personally also prefer it to the orange blossom water.

BOILED CHOCOLATE CAKE (Martha)

Serves 15

1	cup coffee
1	cup sugar
7	ounces semi-sweet chocolate
2	cups walnuts
10	eggs

Separate the eggs. Grind the nuts. Boil the cup of coffee with the sugar and the chocolate. Add the ground nuts, mix well, and bring to a boil once. Add the egg yolks, one by one, mixing well after each addition. Let it cool. Preheat oven to 350°F. Beat egg whites to a peak and carefully incorporate into the nut mixture. Pour it into a greased and floured 9-inch spring form pan, and bake for 1¼ hours. Cool. It can be cut in two circles and filled with any cream, or just frosted with a chocolate glaze.

Cooking Tip:
See recipe for chocolate glaze.

BUTTER DOUGH FOR MANY PURPOSES

Serves 25

2	cups all-purpose flour
8	ounces unsalted butter
2	tablespoons sugar
1	egg
1	tablespoon sour cream
1	dash salt

Mix all of the ingredients to obtain a soft dough. Refrigerate for one hour. Bring the dough to room temperature and divide into two portions. Roll out to the size of a rectangular baking dish. Line the bottom with one half of the dough. Fill it with whatever you like and cover with the other half. Pierce the top with a fork and bake for one hour at 300°F. Let it cool, cut into rhomboids, and sprinkle with powdered sugar.

CHOCOLATE AND ALMOND CAKE

Serves 10

1½	cup blanched almonds
7	ounces bittersweet chocolate
1¼	cups sugar
7	egg whites

Finely chop the almonds and chocolate together in a food processor; add the sugar and mix well. Beat the egg whites stiff and fold into the chocolate/almond mixture. Oil a 9-inch sprin-form pan, and dust it with flour or matzo meal.

Bake in a preheated 300°F oven for one hour, until firm.

Optional is a chocolate-butter frosting.

CHOCOLATE CAKE (Donia)

Serves 15

1	cup sugar
3¾	ounces semi-sweet chocolate
2	cups walnuts
1	tablespoon Cherry Heering
1	tablespoon cognac
1	tablespoon all-purpose flour
1	tablespoon vegetable oil
7	eggs
1	teaspoon vanilla extract

For the frosting

1	cup whipping cream
1	tablespoon sugar
4	ounces semi-sweet chocolate
2	teaspoons instant coffee
	Prepare this the day before baking the cake

Preheat the oven to 350°F. Grease and dust a 9½ inch spring form pan. Melt the chocolate and cool. Beat the egg yolks with sugar to a light color; add vanilla, nuts, cold chocolate, flour, oil, Cherry Heering, and cognac. Beat the egg whites with a dash of salt or cream of tartar. When peaks begin to form, gradually add the sugar (two tablespoons at the time) and continue beating until stiff (but not too stiff). Carefully incorporate the egg whites into the chocolate mixture. Pour into the spring form pan, and bake for approximately forty-five to sixty minutes, or when tester comes out clean.

On low heat, boil the cream, sugar, and chocolate. Refrigerate overnight. The next day, beat the cream and gradually add the coffee. Cut the cake in half, fill it, and decorate with frosting.

CREMESCHNITTEN (Simplified Napoleons)

Half of a 16- or 17-ounce packet frozen puff pastry

Thaw the pastry at room temperature (about 30-40 minutes). Unfold the pastry on a floured surface and cut into three strips, along the fold marks. Cut each strip into four squares. Place the squares onto a greased baking sheet. (Parchment paper is also good.) Bake the pastry at 400°F for 15 minutes or until the pastries are golden brown. Remove from the oven and cool in the baking sheet placed on a wire rack for 15-20 minutes. Split each square into two layers.

For the vanilla filling

1	packet vanilla pudding
1	cup milk
½	cup heavy whipping cream
3	teaspoons powdered sugar
½	teaspoon vanilla extract
½	cup powdered sugar to sprinkle on top.

Mix the pudding with 1 cup of milk and boil until it is creamy. If instant pudding is used, prepare it according to the package directions still using only one cup of milk. Whip the cream with three teaspoons of powdered sugar. When the pudding is completely cold, fold it in the whipped cream.

Put aside eight top squares. Spread 1½ tablespoons of custard on all eight bottom layers; cover with the middle layer, spread another 1½ tablespoons of custard; top and cover with the eight top squares. Sprinkle with powdered sugar and refrigerate.

These Cremeschnitten have to be served immediately or need to be refrigerated for a maximum of six hours.

EASY CHOCOLATE CAKE

Serves 15

8	eggs
4	ounces unsalted butter
1¼	cups sugar
8	ounces semi-sweet chocolate
2½	cups ground almonds with skin
1	teaspoon vanilla extract

Preheat the oven to 250°F. Grease or line (with parchment paper) a 9-inch spring form pan. Separate the eggs. Don't peel the almonds. In an electric mixer, beat the butter with the sugar and egg yolks until no sugar crystals are felt. Melt the chocolate, cool it, and add to the butter mixture. Add the ground almonds and vanilla.

Beat the egg whites to a stiff peak and carefully incorporate it into the chocolate mixture. Pour into the spring form and bake at 250°F for about 30-45 minutes, or until the tester comes out dry. Fill and decorate with any chocolate frosting.

EGG YOLK GLAZED PASTRIES (Dotter Glazur Schnitte)
(My daughter's favorite)

Serves 30

For the dough

2½	cups all-purpose flour
10	ounces unsalted butter,
¾	cup sugar
5	egg yolks
⅓	cup sour cream
2	teaspoons lemon zest
1	cup raspberry jam

For the glaze

1	egg yolk
¾	cup powdered sugar
2	teaspoons lemon juice
¼	cup chocolate sprinkles

Preheat the oven at 370°F. Mix all of the ingredients in an electric mixer. Let the dough rest for 2 hours. Roll out into a ¾-inch thick sheet and line the bottom of a rectangular 12 x 18 inch cookie sheet.

Bake quickly at 375°F for 29 minutes or until light brown. While still hot, spread with jam and then let it cool. Cut into 2-inch wide strips lengthwise and put two strips together.

For the glaze, mix the egg yolk, sugar, and lemon juice, and then bring it to a quick boil. Remove it immediately from the stove and stir all the time. Quickly spread the glaze over each strip of pastry, smoothing it evenly with a knife. While still warm, spread chocolate sprinkles in the center of each strip. Cut strips into small rectangles and put into paper cups.

Cooking Tips:
Butter can be substituted with unsalted margarine.
Sour cream can be substituted with sweet cream.
Raspberry jam can be substituted with red currant or strawberry jam.

FLADEN HUNGARIAN STYLE

Serves 16

For the dough

3	cups all-purpose flour
8	tablespoons unsalted margarine
3	egg yolks
2	tablespoons sugar
1	dash salt

For the filling

1	pound Granny Smith apples, sliced
3	tablespoons honey
5	tablespoons prune butter (lekvar)
¾	cup sugar
¾	cup prepared poppy seeds
1	cup ground walnuts
¼	cup raisins
½	teaspoon cinnamon

Make a dough with the egg yolks, flour, margarine, and sugar. Refrigerate overnight. The next day divide the dough into five parts and roll out equal rectangles or squares, according to size of the baking sheet. Put the first layer at the bottom of a greased and floured lasagna baking dish. Grind the walnuts, scald them in some milk plus two tablespoons of sugar, and spread it over the first sheet. Cover with the second sheet and fill with the prepared poppy seeds, adding some sugar, honey, lemon zest, and juice. (See poppy seeds filling.) Cover with the third sheet pierced with a fork and spread lekvar over it. Cover that with the fourth sheet, and spread on it the peeled and sliced Granny Smith apples scalded in some white wine, mixed with cinnamon and sugar. Cover that with the fifth sheet pierced with a fork.

Preheat the oven at 350°F and bake for one hour, or until the top is light brown. Cool and cut into squares or rectangles; sprinkle with powdered sugar.

FLOURLESS CHOCOLATE TORTE

Serves 15

8	egg yolks
8	ounces unsalted butter
9	ounces semi-sweet chocolate
1¼	cups sugar
2½	cups almonds
1	teaspoon vanilla

Preheat the oven to 250°F. Butter and flour a 9-inch spring form pan, or line it with parchment paper. In an electric mixer, beat the butter, egg yolks, and sugar until no sugar crystals are felt. Toast the almonds slightly and grind them with the skin. Melt and cool the chocolate. Add the vanilla, cooled chocolate, and almonds to the creamed mixture. Beat the 8 egg whites to a peak, and slowly incorporate it into the chocolate mixture. Bake for about 30-45 minutes, or until the tester comes out dry. Cool on a rack. Remove from spring form pan. Cut into 2 parts, fill and decorate with any chocolate frosting.

FLUDEN ROLL (Jewish traditional treat for festivities)

Serves 20

1	package filo sheets
1	cup walnuts
1	cup fine breadcrumbs (made from challah)
1	cup apricot jam
1	cup unsalted butter
1	cup sugar
1	teaspoon cinnamon
½	cup raisins
1	teaspoon lemon (zest)

Thaw and handle the filo sheets according to the package's instructions. Preheat the oven to 300°F. Chop the walnuts, melt the butter, and melt the jam. Crumbs should be made from toasted challah (Jewish braided loaf.) Use four filo sheets for each roll. Brush each sheet with melted butter; on top of the fourth sheet, spread the breadcrumbs, nuts, jam, cinnamon, sugar, raisins, and lemon zest. Roll them into small rolls, brush with butter, and sprinkle them with sugar before baking. Bake at 300°F for 1½ hours, or until it is light brown. Cool on a wire rack and cut the cold rolls into 1 inch wide portions.

Store the rolls in an air-tight cookie jar. They will keep fresh for many months.

Cooking Tips:
Instead of apricot, red currant or rose petals preserves can be used. Instead of lemon zest, orange zest can be used.

FLUDEN (Klara Ostfeld)

Serves 30

For the dough

2½	cups all-purpose flour
7	ounces unsalted butter or margarine
¼	cup sugar
1	egg
1	tablespoon sour cream
1	teaspoon lemon zest

For the filling

1	pound ground walnuts
1	pound sugar
½	cup raisins
¾	cup lemon juice
1	teaspoon lemon zest
	Mix all of the ingredients in a bowl.

Mix by hand or in an electric mixer the butter, flour, egg, sugar, lemon zest, and sour cream to obtain a uniform dough. Divide it into two portions. Grease or line (with parchment paper) a rectangular 9 x 14 inch baking pan. On a floured board, roll out one portion of the dough and place it at the bottom of the pan. With the fingertips, press down the dough and line the sides of the baking pan.

To assemble the fluden

Spread the filling on top of the dough in the baking dish; even it out with the palm of your hands. On wax paper or parchment paper, roll out the second portion and, with the help of the rolling pin, cover the filling. With a fork, push together the borders of the dough until you feel that they are sealed. Pierce the top with a fork in several places.

Preheat the oven to 300°F. Place the baking dish on top of an aluminum tray or heavy foil. Bake it for 1¼ hour, or until the top is golden brown. Remove from the oven and immediately sprinkle with powdered sugar. Let it cool, and with a sharp knife cut out rhomboids of about 4 inches. Remove from pan when it is completely cold.

Cooking Tip:
This fluden can be stored in a closed container and frozen for six months.

FRUIT CAKE

Serves 15

2½	cups all-purpose flour
2	teaspoons baking powder
1	dash salt
1	cup sugar
4	ounces unsalted margarine (or butter)
2	eggs
½	cup sour cream
1	teaspoon lemon zest
	any fruit in season

Sift the dry ingredients. In an electric mixer, blend the margarine with the sugar; add one egg at the time, alternating with the sour cream and flour. Add lemon zest. Fill a 9" spring form pan previously greased and floured. Put any sliced fruit on top and sprinkle with sugar. Bake for 45 minutes at 350°F.

HAZELNUT-CHOCOLATE TORTE (Fanny Glasberg)

Serves 16

8	egg yolks
8	tablespoons unsalted butter
1¼	cups sugar
8	ounces sweet baking chocolate
1½	cups hazelnuts
1	teaspoon vanilla extract
8	egg whites

Separate the eggs. Roast and peel the hazelnuts, and then finely grind them. In an electric mixer, beat the yolks with sugar and butter. Melt the chocolate and let it cool. Add the ground hazelnuts and vanilla to the butter mixture. Beat the egg whites to a peak and incorporate them into the chocolate mixture. Grease and flour a 9" spring form pan and bake at 250°F–300°F until the tester comes out dry. Cool on a rack.

When the torte is completely cold, cut into two circles; fill and ice with any chocolate frosting.

Cooking Tip:
Hazelnuts can be substituted with walnuts or almonds.

HONEY CAKE (My mother's recipe)

Serves 25

4	eggs
1	cup sugar
1	cup honey
3	cups all-purpose flour
1	teaspoon baking soda
½	cup raisins
½	cup walnuts
¾	cup vegetable oil
½	cup strong coffee
4	tablespoons cognac
1	tablespoon lemon zest
½	teaspoon cinnamon or allspice
1	tablespoon lemon juice

Preheat the oven to 250° F. Dissolve the baking soda in the cognac. In a large bowl of an electric mixer, beat the eggs, sugar, lemon zest, juice, coffee, and cinnamon for five minutes. Add the honey, the remaining ingredients, and the flour. Mix well. Oil a deep rectangular baking pan and bake at 250°–300°F for 40-45 minutes, or until the cake tester comes out dry.

HONEY CAKE (Traditional)

Serves 16

1	cup sugar
1	tablespoon vegetable oil
4	eggs
3½	cups all-purpose flour
1	teaspoon baking soda
2	teaspoons baking powder
1	teaspoon ground cloves
1	teaspoon ground ginger
1	teaspoon ground cinnamon
1⅓	cups honey, less 1 tablespoon
1⅓	cups coffee
1	cup walnuts
1	cup raisins

Preheat the oven to 350°F. Grease a 9" spring form pan or a rectangular baking dish. Blend the sugar and oil. Add the eggs and beat well. Sift together the flour, soda, baking powder, and spices. Add alternatively the honey and the coffee, first using the coffee to rinse the honey jar or measuring cup. Stir in nuts and raisins; pour into a baking dish. Bake for 55-60 to sixty minutes. Cool before removing from the pan.

HONEY TORTE (My mother's recipe)

Serves 15

For the bottom

1	tablespoon honey
1	egg
1	tablespoon sugar
1	tablespoon oil
¾	cup all-purpose flour
	Mix the egg, sugar, oil, and flour to make a semi-hard dough

For the top

1¼	cups sugar
1	cup honey (minus 1 tablespoon)
2	cups walnuts
2	ounces semi-sweet chocolate
1	lemon
3	eggs
3	tablespoons fine breadcrumbs
½	cup all-purpose flour
1	teaspoon baking powder

Preheat the oven to 250°-300°F. Melt the chocolate and let it cool. Divide the walnuts; chop one part and grind the other finely. Sift flour with baking powder. Beat the eggs with the sugar to a pale color. Use the zest and juice of one lemon. Add all the other ingredients.

For the bottom

Grease and flour (or line with parchment paper) a 9" spring form pan. Line the bottom with the semi-hard dough, pour the mixture on top, and bake for about 1–1½ hours, or until the top is brown and dry. The cake inside will be moist. Cool and decorate as you like.

LINZER TORTE

Serves 15

For the dough

¼	teaspoon baking powder
1½	cup all-purpose flour
½	cup sugar
½	cup finely ground walnuts or blanched almonds
1	cup tea biscuits crumbs
1	cup unsalted butter
2	hard-cooked egg yolks
¼	teaspoon baking powder
1	tablespoon rum
⅛	teaspoon ground cloves
1	teaspoon lemon zest
1	cup thick red currant or raspberry jam
1	teaspoon vanilla extract
¼	teaspoon cinnamon

For the glaze and finish

2	tablespoons heavy whipping cream
2	raw egg yolks
¼	cup powdered vanilla sugar

This dough needs to be worked very fast. Sift together the flour, cinnamon, cloves, and baking powder. Add the ground nuts, sugar, lemon zest, and mashed egg yolks. With a pastry blender, cut in the butter, raw egg yolks, and vanilla. Work the dough with your hands a bit until it is very smooth. Form a ball, wrap it in plastic or wax paper, and refrigerate for one hour.

Take out the ball and cut off three quarters to work with right away. Return the rest to the refrigerator. Grease and flour a 9-inch spring form pan. Line the bottom and press and push the dough with your fingers to cover the bottom and the sides of the baking pan. The shell should be about ¼ inch thick. If the dough is too firm, let it rest for another few minutes. Spread the red currant jam evenly over the bottom of the shell with the back of a spoon or a spatula.

Take out the remaining dough from the refrigerator and either roll out a nine-inch circle to cover the filled shell, or roll out pieces to form a lattice-like effect. Beat the egg yolk with the cream and brush the top. Refrigerate the unbaked cake for 30 minutes.

Preheat the oven to 350°F and bake the cake for 45-50 minutes, or until the top is light brown. Cool the pan on a rack. Before removing the torte from the pan, make sure the sides don't stick. Carefully release them with a small, sharp knife. Sprinkle generously with the powdered vanilla sugar.

NO BAKE CHEESECAKE (Israeli specialty)

Serves 10

1	packet lemon flavored gelatin
1	teaspoon lemon zest
1	cup water
1	pound farmer cheese
1	cup heavy whipping cream
2	tablespoons sugar
¼	cup cherry or coffee liqueur
¼	cup raisins
10–12	ladyfingers
	chocolate sprinkles for decor

Line a 9" spring form pan with ladyfingers and sprinkle them with the cherry liqueur. Pass the farmer cheese through a strainer; add the sugar, half of the heavy cream, and the lemon zest. Dissolve the packet of lemon gelatin in <u>one</u> cup of hot water; stir well and let it cool. Pour it into the cheese mixture and mix well. Pour the mixture on top of the lady fingers, smooth with a knife, and refrigerate for a few hours or overnight. Whip the remaining heavy cream and decorate the cake. I like to shave a little chocolate on top or use chocolate sprinkles

NO CRUST APPLE PIE

Serves 8

2	pounds apples
1	cup flour
1	teaspoon baking powder
¾	cup sugar
1	cup cream of wheat
9	ounces unsalted butter
1	teaspoon lemon zest
2	teaspoons lemon juice

Peel and grate the tart apples on the large side of grater. Crumble all of the ingredients, like for a streusel; mix in the apples and bake at 350°F for 30-45 minutes, or until the top is brown.

NOODLE TORTE (My mother's recipe)

Serves 14

1	pound thin egg noodles
2	tablespoons cocoa (optional)
1	cup sugar
4	eggs
½	cup golden raisins
1	cup walnuts
½	cup raspberry preserves
1	lemon zest and juice
1	pinch salt
½	teaspoon cinnamon

Cook the noodles al dente in slightly salted water. Drain and rinse them with cold water. Separate the eggs. Coarsely chop the walnuts. Mix the rinsed noodles with the egg yolks and the remaining ingredients. Beat the egg whites to a stiff peak and carefully mix them into the noodles.

This torte can be baked in a spring form pan or in any baking dish previously greased and floured.

Preheat the oven to 350°F and bake for 30-45 minutes. The cake can be topped with meringue when it is almost done or sprinkled with powdered sugar before serving.

Cooking Tips:
Golden raisins are preferred, but dark ones can be used as well.
Use a very good quality of red fruit jam.

NUT CAKE (Aunt Cilly)

Serves 12

6	ounces unsalted butter
¾	cup sugar
5	ounces bitter chocolate
2	cups ground walnuts
6	large eggs
1	teaspoon lemon zest
2–3	tablespoons all-purpose flour or matzo meal
1	teaspoon vanilla extract

Separate eggs. Mix butter, sugar, and egg yolks to a pale color. Melt chocolate and add it to the mixture when cold. Add finely ground walnuts, lemon zest, and vanilla.

Beat egg whites to a peak and carefully incorporate it into the first mixture. Add the flour or matzo meal. Fill a 9" spring form pan and bake at 250°F–300°F for about one hour. Fill and decorate with any frosting or with a chocolate glaze.

PASSOVER CAKE (My son's favorite)

Serves 15

For the bottom

8	egg yolks
1	cup sugar
1½	cups ground walnuts
½	cup vegetable oil
4	ounces semi-sweet chocolate
4	egg whites
1	tablespoon matzo meal

For the top

6	egg whites
¾	cup sugar
1	tablespoon matzo meal
1	cup slivered almonds
1	lemon

Preheat the oven to 300°F. Grease and flour a 9" spring form pan. In an electric mixer, beat the yolks and sugar to a light yellow color. Melt and cool the chocolate and add it together with the remaining ingredients to the egg yolk mixture. Beat the 4 egg whites to a stiff peak and carefully incorporate the walnuts. Bake at 300°F for about a half hour, or until half done.

Beat the six egg whites with the sugar to a stiff peak; add three quarters of a cup of slivered almonds, matzo meal, juice, and zest of one lemon. Pour the meringue on top of the half baked dark part and continue baking for another half hour or until the top is light brown.

PASSOVER NUT CAKE

Serves 12

6	eggs
1	cup sugar
1¾	cups walnuts
1	tablespoon matzo meal
2	tablespoons strong coffee
2	tablespoons water
½	cup apricot jam
1	cup whipped cream

Separate the eggs. In an electric mixer, beat the egg yolks with sugar to a pale color. Add all other ingredients and mix slowly but thoroughly. Beat the egg whites to a peak and carefully fold them into the first mixture. Bake at 375°F for about 40 minutes. Test for doneness, but the cake should be a bit moist. Cool and cut in half. Spread apricot jam between the two circles and the top. Decorate with either whipping cream or a coffee cream. (See recipes.)

PASSOVER SPONGE CAKE (Hanna Muller)

Serves 12

12	eggs
1	cup matzo cake meal
¼	cup corn starch
1½	cups sugar
½	cup orange juice
2	teaspoons lemon zest

Separate the eggs and mix the sugar and egg yolks to a pale color. Add the lemon zest and orange juice. Sift the cake meal and corn starch. Beat the egg whites to a stiff peak and carefully mix them into the first mixture.

Use a chiffon cake mold plus another small mold. Fill just three quarters of the chiffon mold and put the rest in the smaller mold. Bake at 325°F for one hour or until a tester comes out dry.

POPPY SEED ROLL

Serves 24

For the dough

3	envelopes granulated yeast
½	cup lukewarm water
½	cup milk
12	tablespoons unsalted butter
1½	teaspoons salt
6	cups all-purpose flour
2	teaspoons lemon zest
3	tablespoons heavy dark rum
5	egg yolks
3	eggs
3	tablespoons heavy cream

For the filling

½	pound poppy seeds
½	cup honey
¼	cup melted butter
½	cup heavy whipping cream
½	cup chopped raisins
2	teaspoons lemon zest
¼	teaspoon cinnamon
¼	teaspoon nutmeg
½	cup chopped walnuts

For the egg wash

2	egg yolks
2	tablespoons heavy cream

Preheat the oven to 350°F. In a small bowl, combine the yeast, ½ a cup of lukewarm water, and a ¼ cup of sugar. Mix lightly and set aside for 5 minutes. Scald milk with butter, a ¼ cup of sugar, and salt. Stir until the butter is melted. Cool slightly and pour into a large bowl. Add tw2 cups of flour, yeast, lemon zest, and rum. Beat with a wooden spoon for two minutes by hand, or for 30 seconds in an electric mixer. Add the egg yolks, whole eggs, and the remaining flour. Beat until a smooth dough is formed. You may need between 6-7 cups flour.

Turn the dough onto a floured board and knead for 5-7 minutes, or beat for 4 minutes in mixer with a hook. If the dough feels sticky, you may have to add small amounts of flour. The dough should be very smooth and elastic with blisters on the surface. Shape the dough into a ball and place into a large, well-buttered bowl. Turn the dough once to coat it with butter, cover the bowl, and let the dough rise in a warm place for about 1–1½ hours, or until it is doubled in bulk.

Preheat oven to 350º F. Punch down the dough; place on a floured board and knead it lightly for 2 minutes. Divide the dough into 2 parts. Roll out one part into a rectangle to about a ¼-inch thickness; fill it with poppy seed filling and the other half with walnut filling. Spread the filling over the dough, leaving a two-inch border free of filling. Roll up in a jelly roll fashion and seal the ends and along the seam. Turn the seam down and form it into a horseshoe, or just leave it like a strudel. Butter a jelly roll pan and sprinkle it with flour. Slide the strudels off the board onto the pan. Let it rise covered until double in bulk. Brush the dough with egg wash and bake in for 50-55 minutes, or until golden brown.

Walnut filling

2	cups ground walnuts
½	cup sugar
½	cup apricot preserves
½	cup heavy cream
¼	cup dark rum
½	cup raisins

In a saucepan, combine the walnuts, sugar, apricot preserves, and cream. Cook for 5 minutes, stirring constantly. Combine the rum and raisins. Let it stand for te10 minutes, and then add it to the nut mixture. Cool completely.

Poppy seed filling

1	jar "Baker" poppy seed filling
½	cup apricot preserves
½	cup raisins
½	cup dark rum
½	cup crushed walnuts

Combine the prepared filling with the apricot preserves. Soak the raisins in rum for a few minutes, and then add them to the poppy seeds with the walnuts. Use this filling the same way as the nut filling.

(SEE OTHER POPPY SEEDS FILLING)

POPPY SEED CAKE I

Serves 15

4	large eggs
5	ounces unsalted butter or margarine
1½	cups poppy seeds
½	cup all-purpose flour
½	cup potato starch
3	tablespoons milk
1	teaspoon baking powder
1	tablespoon Grand Marnier or any liqueur

Mix all of the ingredients, and bake them in 9" spring form pan at 350°F, or until a tester comes out dry. Decorate with whipping cream or any frosting you like.

POPPY SEED CAKE II (Aunt Cilly)

Serves 15

9	ounces unsalted butter
1¼	pounds walnuts
1½	cups poppy seeds
2	cups sugar
10	eggs
7	ounces unsweetened chocolate
1	teaspoon vanilla extract
1	lemon
3	tablespoons all-purpose flour

Preheat the oven to 250°F. Grind the poppy seeds. Separate the eggs. Melt the chocolate and let it cool. Beat the egg yolks with half of the sugar to a pale cream. Add butter and all the other ingredients. Grate the rind of one lemon, squeeze the juice, and add it to the chocolate mixture.

Beat the egg whites with the remaining sugar to a stiff peak and slowly add two to three tablespoons of flour. Incorporate it carefully into the chocolate batter. Butter and dust with flour a 9" spring form pan; fill with the mixture and bake at 250°F for the first ten minutes, and then increase to 350°F for about one hour, or when a tester comes out dry. The cake can be decorated with a chocolate frosting or whipped cream.

SCHMETTENTORTE
(A Bukovina specialty, my mother's version)

Serves 18

For the dough

2	cups all-purpose flour
½	cup sugar
1	teaspoon vanilla extract or 1 packet vanilla sugar
1¼	cups ground walnuts
½	teaspoon baking soda
1¾	sticks unsalted butter (14 tablespoons)
1	egg

For the cream

¾	cup sugar
1¼	cups ground walnuts
1	cup sour cream
1	teaspoon vanilla extract
1	teaspoon lemon juice
1	tablespoon cocoa (optional)

Sift the flour with the baking soda. In an electric mixer, mix the cream, butter, sugar, egg, and vanilla, and then gradually add the flour. Divide the dough it into 4 equal balls, and roll them out to fit the bottoms of four greased and floured 9-inch spring form pans. Pierce with a fork all around and bake at 350°F, or until light golden brown. Let it cool. The layers have to be baked in advance.

In a saucepan, mix the sour cream, walnuts, vanilla, lemon juice, and sugar. Bring it to a light boil. Let it cool. Fill the layers with cream and decorate with the same, sprinkled with chopped walnuts or with whipping cream.

Variations:
1. Spread apricot jam on each layer before spreading the nut cream.
2. Use drained sour cherries from a can mixed with whipping cream between layers before filling with the nut cream. This cake tastes best if used a couple of days later.
3. Add one tablespoon of cocoa to the sour cream filling.

TIRAMISU À LA RUTH GOLD

Serves 20

1	box Graham crackers
1	14-oz can sweetened condensed milk.
5	egg yolks
1	cup milk
1	package ladyfingers

For the chocolate cream

3	tablespoons cocoa
1	tablespoon cognac
2	tablespoons sugar
5	tablespoons black coffee

For the icing

1	cup heavy whipping cream
4	teaspoons powdered sugar

In a rectangular Pyrex, or equivalent serving dish, line the bottom with Graham crackers sprinkled with black coffee. Separate eggs and mix the egg yolks with the condensed milk and regular milk, and bring them to a boil. Lower the heat and stir constantly with a wire whisk until the cream feels like a pudding. Cool and pour evenly over the crackers.

Mix together the cocoa, coffee, cognac, and sugar. Bring to a boil and, on low heat, stir constantly until slightly thickened. Remove from the stove and while still warm, dip each ladyfinger quickly in the chocolate cream and lay them on top of the egg cream. Decorate with whipped cream and sprinkle with chocolate sprinkles or grated chocolate. Refrigerate overnight. Cut into squares before serving.

TORT ALCAZAR (Romanian specialty)

Serves 15

6	egg whites
1	cup sugar
2	cups hazelnuts or walnuts
2	tablespoons fine breadcrumbs

For the filling

6	egg yolks
⅔	cup sugar
2	tablespoons instant coffee powder
¼	cup water
7	ounces unsalted butter

Roast and peal the hazelnuts. Divide them into two portions. Chop one portion and grind the other finely. Beat the egg whites with a dash of salt, adding the sugar gradually until peaks form. Carefully mix in the nuts and the breadcrumbs. Grease and flour (or line with parchment paper) a rectangular baking dish (lasagna size). Preheat the oven to 275°F and bake for 20-30 minutes, or until a tester comes out dry. Cool on a rack. It can also be baked in a 9-inch spring form pan and cut into two halves when cold.

Dissolve the coffee in the ¼ cup water. In a double boiler, mix the egg yolks with the sugar and the dissolved coffee. Whisk constantly until the mixture turns creamy; do not boil it. Separately, foam the butter and add the cooled cream, mixing well. Cut the cooled sheet lengthwise into 3 equal parts, and fill and decorate with the same cream. Cut square portions.

Cooking Tip:
The same cake can be baked in a 9-inch spring form pan, cut into half, and filled with the same cream.

WALNUT CAKE

Serves 15

For the bottom

4½	tablespoons unsalted butter
9	tablespoons all-purpose flour
1	tablespoon vinegar
1	tablespoon sugar

For the top

7	eggs
1¾	cups walnuts
1	cup sugar
2	teaspoons lemon juice
2	teaspoons lemon zest
1	teaspoon vanilla

Make a dough with the butter, flour, vinegar, and sugar. Grease and flour a 9" spring form pan and put the dough at the bottom.

Separate eggs and mix 5 egg yolks with the sugar until pale. Separately beat the 7 egg whites stiff and mix carefully with the yolk mixture, adding vanilla, lemon zest, juice, and walnuts. Pour the mixture on top of the bottom layer and bake at 300°F for 30-40 minutes, or when a tester comes out dry. Decorate with any cream of your liking, or just with whipping cream.

YEAST CAKE (Lucie Sadmon)

Serves 15

6	ounces unsalted margarine or butter
2	eggs
3½	cups all-purpose flour
½	cup milk
½	cup sugar
1	teaspoon vanilla extract
1	teaspoon lemon zest
1½	packet dry yeast
1	dash salt
½	cup sour cream

Dissolve the yeast in lukewarm milk. Add a dash of sugar, a dash of flour, and let the dough rise to double the size. In a food processor or electric mixer, combine the margarine, sugar, eggs, half the amount of flour, and the sour cream. Mix well and add the rest of the flour and the dissolved yeast mixture. Put the dough into a bowl and cover, or seal in a plastic bag and refrigerate overnight. The next day knead the dough for a few minutes, roll it out into a rectangle, and fill it with anything you like, i.e., walnut filling, poppy seed filling, etc. (See respective recipes.)

Cooking Tip:
Instead of margarine, unsalted butter can be used.

CREAMS AND FROSTINGS

CHOCOLATE FROSTING I

½   cup unsalted butter
3   cups powdered sugar
3   tablespoons cocoa
4   tablespoons heavy cream
1   teaspoon vanilla

Beat all ingredients in an electric mixer to a fluffy consistency. Fill and ice cakes with this frosting.

CHOCOLATE FROSTING II

6	tablespoons unsalted butter
2	tablespoons light corn syrup
1	teaspoon vanilla extract
2	oz. unsweetened chocolate
2	cups confectioners' sugar
1	tablespoon milk

Have the butter at room temperature. Melt the chocolate. In a small bowl of an electric mixer with the paddle attachment, beat the butter until creamy. Add the corn syrup and keep mixing. Add the melted and cooled chocolate, the vanilla, and slowly add the sugar. Continue beating until the mixture begins to thicken. Add the milk and beat until the frosting has a spreadable consistency.

CHOCOLATE FROSTING III

¼   cup cocoa

1   cup granulated sugar

¼   cup unsalted butter

¼   cup milk

1   teaspoon vanilla

Mix all of the ingredients together. Bring to a boil for one minute. Add vanilla. Cool partially, and then beat with a mixer for 3 minutes to obtain a spreadable consistency.

CHOCOLATE GLAZE

4   ounces sweet baker's chocolate

3   tablespoons water

3   tablespoons unsalted butter

Break the chocolate into small pieces, add water, and melt over low heat, stirring constantly. Remove it from the heat, stirring in the butter. Cool it to thicken if necessary. Pour over cake and garnish as desired.

CHOCOLATE BUTTER FROSTING (Aunt Cilly)

4	egg yolks
¼	cup sugar
2	tablespoons whole milk
4	ounces semi-sweet chocolate
8	ounces unsalted butter
2	tablespoons strong coffee

Separate the eggs, break the chocolate into small pieces, and heat all of the ingredients in a double boiler, stirring constantly. Do not bring cream to a boil. Cool and add the butter. Beat in an electric mixer until foamy.

CHOCOLATE FILLING FOR TORTE WAFERS (Oblatten)

5	wafers
½	cup sugar
1	egg yolk
¾	cup hazelnuts
5	tablespoons unsalted butter
5	ounces semi-sweet chocolate
1	teaspoon vanilla extract

Use five round or square torte wafers. Roast, peel, and finely grind hazelnuts (walnuts or almonds can be used). Cream butter and sugar until no grains are felt. Melt and cool the chocolate, and add it with the yolk and vanilla to the butter mixture. Take out some cream for frosting. Add the hazelnuts to the remaining mixture.

Fill the wafers, leaving the top one without frosting. Cover them with a heavy plate, put some weight on top, and refrigerate overnight. The next day, decorate with the remaining chocolate cream.

CHOCOLATE GANACHE I (Cake frosting)

1   cup heavy cream

½   pound semi-sweet chocolate

A day ahead of baking the cake, bring the cream to a boil in a medium pot over high heat. Remove it from the stove and stir in the finely chopped chocolate. Stir rapidly until all of the chocolate has melted and the mixture is smooth. Cool to room temperature, stirring constantly. Cover the ganache and refrigerate it overnight. The next day, whip the ganache in a chilled bowl of an electric mixer until peaks form.

CHOCOLATE GANACHE II

8	ounces semi-sweet chocolate
¾	cup heavy whipping cream
2	tablespoons unsalted butter
1	tablespoon cognac

Heat the cream over medium heat or in microwave oven for two minutes. Pour over the chocolate, stir in the butter, and mix well. Let it cool before frosting a cake.

MOCHA CREAM FROSTING

6	egg yolks
2	tablespoons instant coffee
¾	cup sugar
¼	cup water
8	ounces unsalted butter

Dissolve the coffee in the water. Whisk the yolks with all of the ingredients, except the butter, in a double boiler until it is creamy. Separately foam the butter, and add it to the cooled creamy mixture.

WHIPPED CREAM TOPPING

1 cup heavy whipping cream
4 teaspoons powdered sugar
1 tablespoon cold water
½ teaspoon unflavored gelatin

Before whipping, chill the small bowl and beaters of an electric mixer. Sprinkle the gelatin over the cold water in a small heatproof glass or cup. Let rest for a few minutes and then put the glass in a pan with hot water on moderate heat until gelatin is dissolved. Remove from stove and cool. Reserve 2 tablespoons of cream for later. In the chilled bowl, beat the cream wit the sugar until it almost begins to thicken. Now stir the reserved cream into the dissolved gelatin and beat into the cream. Continue beating until mixture holds a shape.

Cookies

BOW TIES (Spitzbuben)

Serves 18

1¼	cups all-purpose flour
2	eggs
3	egg yolks
3	tablespoons unsalted butter
2	tablespoons granulated sugar
1	teaspoon lemon zest
1	tablespoons rum or brandy
1	cup's confectioners' sugar for sprinkling
1½	cups vegetable oil for frying
2	tablespoons sugar
2	tablespoons heavy whipping cream or sour cream
½	teaspoon salt

Beat the eggs with the egg yolks to a light color. Beat in the sugar, heavy cream, salt, and brandy. Add the flour. The dough will be soft. Knead it on a floured board until smooth. Cover with plastic and let it rest for fifteen minutes. With a rolling pin, roll out the dough to about ⅛ - inch thickness. Cut off a small piece at a time, as this dough dries very fast. Cut out long strips about 1½ inches wide, and then cut each strip into 2½ inch pieces. Cut a slit in the center, and pull the one end through the slit to form a loose loop. You can also twist the strip in the center, like a bow. Cover the shaped bows until they are ready to fry. Heat the oil in a deep pan to 375°F, and fry the bows, a few at a time, turning them once until slightly browned. Drain the dough on paper towels. Sprinkle with confectioners' sugar.

CHEESE DOUGH CRESCENTS (Kipferl)

Serves 20

2	cups flour
8	ounces unsalted butter
8	ounces farmer cheese
1	dash salt

Mix all ingredients to a soft dough.

Roll out the dough to about one inch thick; make a round circle and cut out triangles. Fill them with jam, nuts, sugar, or any other filling; roll up. Glaze it with one egg yolk, place on a greased cookie sheet, turning both ends down to form a crescent. Bake at 350°F until it is light brown.

CHOCOLATE STREET COOKIES

Serves 20

1¼	cups all-purpose flour
¼	teaspoon baking powder
¼	teaspoon cinnamon
1	pinch salt
8	ounces semi-sweet chocolate
1	tablespoon butter
2	eggs
¾	cup sugar
½	teaspoon vanilla extract
¾	cup walnuts

In an electric mixer, beat the eggs at a high speed; gradually add the sugar and continue mixing for four to five minutes. Chop the nuts. Melt the chocolate in double boiler and cool; add this to the egg mixture and add the remaining ingredients.

Line a large cookie sheet with parchment paper, and place one teaspoon full for each cookie. Leave a 1½ inch space between them. Bake in preheated oven at 350°F for about 12 minutes. Don't bake much longer, or they will be too dry.

CREAM CHEESE PASTRY

Serves 24

1	cup unsalted butter
8	ounces cream cheese (can be low fat)
1	teaspoon vanilla extract
1	dash salt
2¼	cups all-purpose flour
¼	cup powdered sugar

Have the butter and cheese at room temperature. In an electric mixer, cream the cheese, butter, and vanilla. Sift the flour and gradually add it to the cheese mixture until the dough forms a ball. If the dough is too sticky, add more flour. Wrap it in plastic and refrigerate overnight.

Cooking Tip:
This dough can be used for crescents, pies, or rugelach.

FLORENTINE COOKIES

Serves 20

2	cups walnuts
5	egg whites
1	cup sugar
4	ounces semi-sweet chocolate for filling

Preheat the oven to 250°F. Finely grind the walnuts. Make a dough with 2 egg whites, with the walnuts and ¾ of the 1 cup sugar. Beat the remaining 3 egg whites with the remaining ¼ cup of sugar to a stiff peak and fold it into the nut dough. With a spoon, drop the mixture onto a cookie sheet and bake until dry. Cool. Put two together with melted semi-sweet chocolate.

FLUDEN (Martha)

This is a traditional Eastern European Jewish delicacy that I call the "Jewish Baklava."

Serves 25

4	cups walnuts
1¼	cup sugar (less 5 tablespoons)
¾	cups golden raisins
½	cup fine breadcrumbs
½	cup lemon juice
2	eggs
7	sheets filo dough
2	tablespoons honey
2	tablespoons vegetable oil

Crush the nuts with a rolling pin, or chop coarsely. Take out 5 tablespoons of sugar from the 1¼ cup. Mix together the remaining ingredients. Divide the filling into three portions.

Oil a lasagna baking sheet well and cover with one filo sheet sprinkled with oil and crumbs, and then cover with another sheet. Spread ⅓ of the filling on the sheet and even it out with your hand. Drizzle with one tablespoon honey and one tablespoon of crumbs. Cover with the second sheet of filo dough, sprinkle again with oil, spread the second part of the filling, and repeat the honey and oil procedure. Cover with a third sheet and spread the last third of filling; sprinkle with honey and crumbs. Cover with one more filo sheet sprinkled with oil and sugar. Cover with the last filo sheet and press it down with the palm of your hand. Sprinkle one handful of sugar on top and cut about a quarter of an inch around the edges before cutting it into one-inch long strips, and then cutting diagonally so as to obtain rhomboids.

Cover with a brown (bag) paper and bake at 350°F for one hour, or until edges are light brown.

Cool on a rack and cut out portions. Put in paper cupcake holders and store in an airtight box for several weeks. The Fluden can be frozen for one year.

GIANT CHOCOLATE CHIP COOKIES

Serves 16

2	cups all-purpose flour
1½	teaspoons baking soda
1	teaspoon salt
1	cup unsalted butter
1	cup granulated sugar
¾	cup packed light brown sugar
2	eggs
2	teaspoons vanilla extract
12	ounces chocolate chips or bars
1	cup pecans

Heat the oven to 375°F. Divide the flour. Sift 1¾ cup flour with the baking soda and salt. In another bowl, beat the butter and sugar with an electric mixer until all crystals are dissolved, for about five minutes. Add eggs one at the time, beating well after each addition. At low speed, add the dry ingredients, mixing only until well blended. Beat in vanilla.

Toss the remaining ¼ cup of flour with the chopped chocolate or chips and the finely chopped nuts; stir them into the dough by hand. Using a quarter cup scoop or measure, drop the dough onto non-stick cookie sheets, 4 inches apart (4 to a sheet)

Bake 2 sheets at a time for 15-18 minutes, rotating pans halfway through. Allow the cookies to cool for 2 minutes on pans before carefully moving them with a large spatula to wire racks in order to cool completely. The batch makes 16 giant cookies.

GRANDMA'S COOKIES (Kichalech, a Jewish specialty)

Serves 30

3	eggs
½	cup vegetable oil
½	cup sugar
2	tablespoons milk
½	teaspoon baking powder
1	pound all-purpose flour
1	teaspoon vanilla extract
1	tablespoon Cointreau

Mix all of the ingredients. On the kneading board, sprinkled with plenty of sugar, roll out small batches of dough and cut out with a glass or cookie cutter. Grease a large baking sheet with oil and bake at 275°F until they are golden (about 30 minutes).

The cookies can be kept for a long time in a tightly closed box.

HAMANTASCHEN (Haman ears; a Purim treat)

Serves 20

5	ounces unsalted butter
2	tablespoons sugar
1¼	cups all-purpose flour
¼	teaspoon vanilla extract
1	egg yolk
2	teaspoons milk
1	egg, lightly beaten, to glaze

See poppy seed filling.
See povidla/plum filling.

Mix the flour with the salt, sugar, and vanilla extract. Cut the butter into small pieces and rub it into the flour. Mix in the egg yolk and press it all into a ball. Work very briefly adding a little (2-3 tablespoons) milk if necessary to bind the dough. Wrap in plastic wrap and refrigerate for one hour. On a floured board knead well and then roll out to ⅛" thickness. Cut out rounds about 2 ½ " in diameter. Place one heaping teaspoon of the filling on each round. Pinch together three sides of the round to form a triangle and place on a greased cookie sheet. Brush with the beaten egg. Bake at 375 degrees F. for 15-20 minutes, or until golden brown.

Cooking Tip:
Instead of poppy seeds, prune filling can be used (prune butter, lekvar, or homemade).

KICHALECH (A Jewish specialty)

Serves 30

4	eggs
2	tablespoons vegetable oil
⅛	teaspoon salt
2	tablespoons sugar
2¾	cups all-purpose flour
2	tablespoons dark rum

For topping:

½	cup sugar

Beat the eggs with the oil, salt, and two tablespoons of sugar for one minute. Add the flour; just enough to make a very soft dough that will be slightly sticky. Let the dough rest for thirty minutes.

Preheat the oven to 400°F. Place the dough on a well floured board and form a ball. Gently roll out a circle to about a ¼ - inch thick. Grease a cookie sheet with plenty of oil and dip every cookie in the oil on both sides. Sprinkle with sugar and bake at 400°F for fifteen minutes; lower to 350°F and continue baking for another 25 minutes. Cookies should be golden and dry. Test for dryness.

Cooking Tip:
The cookies can be kept for two weeks in a tightly closed box.

LINZER SQUARES (Linzerschnitte)

Serves 20

1½	cup walnuts
1	cup unsalted butter
1	cup sugar
3	cups flour
2	teaspoon lemon zest
2	teaspoon orange zest
3	eggs
2	teaspoons baking powder
1	pinch salt
¾	cup jam (any red berry)
1	egg for brushing

Mix all of the ingredients quickly in a food processor or electric mixer. Leave one third of the dough for lattice, or for a top layer. Preheat the oven to 350°F.

Line a lasagna baking sheet, or any other deep baking pan, with parchment paper or grease and sprinkle lightly with flour. Roll out the dough to fit the bottom of the pan; spread jam on top. From the saved dough, create a lattice. Beat one egg lightly and brush the lattice; cover with slivered almonds or chopped walnuts.

Bake until light brown. Cool and cut into squares or rhomboids.

Cooking Tips:
Any red berry preserves can be used.

If you don't want to make a lattice, simply roll out the reserved dough and lay it on top of the jam. Brush with egg and sprinkle with slivered walnuts.

LINZER TARTLETS

Serves 20

1	cup unsalted butter
½	cup sugar
½	cup bread flour
½	cup all-purpose flour
2	egg yolks
¼	cup ground, blanched almonds or walnuts
1	teaspoon vanilla extract or one tablespoon vanilla sugar
1	pinch salt
1	teaspoon lemon zest
1	egg
½	cup strawberry jam, or any other red jam
½	cup confectioners' sugar

Mix all of the ingredients quickly. Divide the mixture in half. Roll out the first portion on a floured surface and cut out rounds of 2 ¾" in diameter. Roll out a second portion and cut out the same amount and size of cookies, but these have to be pierced with a special cookie cutter so as to make 3 holes. (There are special cookie cutters for these tartlets.)

Bake at 350°F until golden brown. Cool and spread jam on the whole cookie. Sprinkle the perforated cookie with confectioners' sugar and put it on top of the jam-covered ones.

LONDONER SCHNITTE

Serves 30

For the dough

3	cups all-purpose flour
½	cup sugar
¾	cup unsalted butter
3	eggs yolks

For the topping

1	teaspoon lemon zest
3	egg whites
¼	cup sugar
½	cup apricot preserves
1	cup ground walnuts
2	tablespoons cocoa

In an electric mixer or food processor, mix the sugar, butter, yolks, and flour to a soft dough. Line a deep cookie sheet with parchment paper and spread the dough to about a half an inch high. Pierce with a fork and bake at 350°F until the edges are slightly brown (half baked) and cool. Spread apricot or raspberry preserves over the half baked dough.

Beat the egg whites with the sugar until stiff, but not dry. Carefully mix in the walnuts, the lemon zest and the cocoa. Cover the half-baked dough with the beaten egg white and return it to the oven to bake for about another ½ hour, or until the top is golden brown. Cool on a rack and cut into squares or rhomboids.

MACAROONS FOR PASSOVER

Serves 30

1	cup sugar
½	lemon
2	egg whites
1	teaspoon lemon juice
2	tablespoons matzo meal
1½	cups ground walnuts

Use a food processor. Process the sugar with the rind of half a lemon and add the remaining ingredients. Form small balls and put half a walnut on top of each. Line a cookie sheet with parchment paper moistened with oil. Bake at 325°F for 25 minutes.

MANDELBROT (Jewish-style biscotti)

Serves 50

4–5	eggs
¾	cup vegetable oil
1	cup sugar
1	pinch salt
1	teaspoon vanilla extract
1½	cups ground walnuts
1	teaspoon lemon zest
1	teaspoon orange zest
2	tablespoons raspberry preserves
2	teaspoons baking powder
4	cups all-purpose flour
½	cup raisins
¾	cup vegetable oil
1	egg yolk for glaze

Soak the raisins for a few minutes and dry with a paper towel. Preheat the oven to 350°F.

Sift the flour with the salt and baking powder. In an electric mixer, beat the eggs with the sugar to a pale cream. Add the oil, lemon, orange, zest and vanilla, and beat them to a light emulsion. Now blend in the flour, coarsely chopped nuts, and preserves. Add the flour gradually to obtain a soft dough. If it is too sticky, add more flour. With oily hands, form 3-4 slim long rolls. Place them onto a greased cookie sheet, a few inches apart. Brush with egg yolk and bake for 15-20 minutes until they are hard and light brown.

Remove the rolls from the oven, let them cool and cut into diagonal slices about ½ inch thick. Put the slices back on the sheets and bake at 300°F for 10-15 minutes, turning them once. Turn off the oven, but leave the biscotti inside to dry some more.

The biscotti will keep fresh for a couple of months in a well-sealed box.

Cooking Tips:
Strawberry jam can be also used. Rose petals jam is preferred to raspberry jam.
Substitute walnuts with blanched, slightly roasted and coarsely chopped almonds.
Raisins can be substituted with dried cranberries.

MATZOH FARFEL CANDIES (A Passover treat)

Serves 20

½	pound matzo farfel
1	whole egg
1	pound honey
½	cup sugar
1	cup coarsely chopped walnuts

Mix the farfel with the beaten egg until it is well absorbed. Boil the honey and the sugar to obtain a syrup, stirring it until it is light brown. Add the nuts and the farfel and continue to simmer on low heat, stirring it until it turns medium brown and all the syrup is absorbed.

Wet a smooth surface (marble is best, but mica will do) and turn the mixture onto it. Wet the palms of your hands and flatten the candy dough to ¾ inch thick. Allow it to cool completely. Cut the dough into diamond shapes and place them in paper muffin cups.

MERINGUES (Luba Hochner)

Serves 20

4	egg whites
1	cup granulated sugar
⅓	cup powdered sugar
1	tablespoon cornstarch
½	cup ground walnuts

Beat the egg whites with sugar and powdered sugar until they are very stiff. Add the nuts and mix well. On a cookie sheet, lined with parchment paper, drop teaspoons full of mixture, or use a decorating bag. Bake at 250°F at first, and then lower the temperature to 225°F for one to two hours, or until the meringues are dry.

Cooking Tip:
Substitute powdered sugar with one tablespoon of cornstarch.

PISCHINGER SCHNITTE
(Filled torte wafers, an Austrian specialty)

Serves 20

5	torte wafers
1	cup marble halvah
1	tablespoon strong instant coffee
¼	cup water
½	cup sugar
3	tablespoons cocoa
1	teaspoon Kahlua liquor
8	ounces unsalted margarine or butter
1	teaspoon vanilla extract

Dissolve the instant coffee in the water and heat with the halvah, sugar, vanilla, and cocoa on very low heat. Stir well and add the Kahlua and the margarine. While still warm, spread the mixture over four of the wafers, leaving about a ¼ of a cup for icing later. Place a heavy plate or other object on top of the filled wafers and refrigerate for a few hours. Take out and decorate with the remaining cream. Cut the wafers into squares or triangles.

POPPY SEED COOKIES (Dora Fleminger)

Serves 20

2	cups all-purpose flour
2	teaspoons baking powder
2	egg yolks
¾	cup sugar
1	teaspoon vanilla extract
1	orange
1	pinch salt
1	teaspoon rum
½	cup vegetable oil
4	tablespoons poppy seeds

Squeeze the juice from a small orange. Separate the eggs and mix the yolks with the sugar, vanilla, orange juice, rum, and salt. Sift the flour with the baking powder and add this to the egg mixture, alternating with the oil. Add the poppy seeds. On a floured board, knead the dough to a soft ball, and then divide it in half. Cover the other half with plastic. Roll out a sheet of dough approximately ½ inch thick. Cut out any cookie pattern you like and place the dough on a large cookie sheet lined with parchment paper. Place the cookies in a cold oven and heat it up to 350°F. Bake for about ½ hour, or until they are light brown. They can be kept for a few weeks in a tightly closed box.

Cooking Tip:
Instead of rum, cognac or whiskey can be used.
You can also mix half whole wheat flour with half all-purpose flour.
Instead of oil, a half a cup of unsalted butter can be used.

POPPY SEED COOKIES (Traditional)

Serves 40

½	cup unsalted butter
¾	cup sugar
2	eggs
½	teaspoon vanilla extract
½	teaspoon lemon zest
⅓	cup poppy seeds
2	cups all-purpose flour
2	teaspoons baking powder
¼	teaspoon salt

In an electric mixer, cream the butter with the sugar until a light color is obtained. Add eggs and vanilla, lemon zest and poppy seeds. Beat another 5 minutes. Sift together the dry ingredients and add them to the first mixture; mix well. Chill the dough for about one hour. Roll into a ½ -inch thickness. Cut out cookies of any shape. Place cookies on a lightly greased cookie sheet and bake for 10-15 minutes, or until they are light brown.

Cooking Tips:
Instead of butter, ½ a cup of vegetable oil can be used.
You can use 1 cup of whole wheat flour and 1 cup all-purpose flour if you'd like.

POPPY SEED CRESCENTS (Aunt Cilly)

Serves 20

3	cups all-purpose flour
3	sticks unsalted butter
3	egg yolks
1	pinch salt
2	tablespoons white vinegar

For the filling: See poppy seed filling

Mix half of the flour with the butter. Mix the other half with the 3 egg yolks, vinegar, and salt. Mix the two together and beat the dough with the rolling pin several times on a floured hard surface.

Prepare the poppy seed filling, or buy the commercial one. Roll out the dough into a round circle and cut it into triangles. Fill the triangles with the poppy seed mixture at the edges and roll them up and curve the ends into a ½ moon shape. Brush with egg yolk and bake at 350°F, or until the top is brownish.

PUFF PASTRY RUGELACH

Serves 30

2	sheets puff pastry
1	egg

For the filling

1	lemon
½	cup sugar
¼	cup raisins
¼	pound walnuts

Thaw the puff pastry and roll it out very thin. Use the zest and juice of one lemon. Mix all of the ingredients and spread it on the dough. Roll it like a strudel, or cut out small triangles to create crescents. Brush with egg. Bake at 350°F for 30-35 minutes.

Cooking Tip:
Other fillings could be: apricot jam plus coconut, sugar and lemon zest, or cocoa, sugar, nuts, and cinnamon.

STRUDEL DOUGH (Lucie Sadmon)

Serves 20-24

3	cups all-purpose flour
2	teaspoons baking powder
1	cup sour cream
8	ounces unsalted butter
1	pinch salt
1	egg yolk for glaze

Sift the flour with salt and baking powder. Mix all of the ingredients in a food processor or electric mixer, and let the dough rest overnight. Take out the next day, and let it reach room temperature. Divide it into four equal parts. While rolling out the first part, cover the remaining dough. Roll out like a strudel and fill it with anything you desire. Brush the top with egg yolk and bake at 350 F, or until top is light brown. It can also be made like a square pie.

Cooking Tip:
Butter can be substituted with unsalted margarine.

Instead of one cup sour cream, half buttermilk and half sour cream can be used.

Variations of sweet fillings
1. Jam, nuts, sugar, breadcrumbs, raisins, and lemon zest
2. Cocoa, nuts, sugar, breadcrumbs, and raisins
3. ½ cup sugar, 1 cup ground walnuts, apricot or orange jam, lemon juice and a zest
4. ½ cup sugar, 1 cup walnuts or almonds, ¼ cup raisins, and 1 teaspoon lemon zest

Spread the breadcrumbs first, and then all the other ingredients. Roll like a strudel. Place on a baking sheet, brush with egg yolk, and bake at 350°F until the top is brownish.

SUGAR BOWS/EGG TWISTS

Serves 16

½	teaspoon vanilla
1	teaspoon sugar
2⅓	cups flour
5	large eggs
¾	cup vegetable oil
1	teaspoon salt
1	cup sugar for rolling

Place eggs, oil, sugar, flour, and salt in a large bowl of an electric mixer fitted with a paddle. Mix at low speed and then increase to high speed for 5 minutes.

Remove the paddle and scrape the batter down the sides of the bowl. Cover and let the dough rest at room temperature for one hour. It should feel soft and spongy outside. Remove the dough from the bowl and make a ball. (It will feel sticky.) Preheat the oven to 350°F. Grease 2 cookie sheets.

Sprinkle a work surface with 1 cup of sugar, about ⅛ "high. Place the dough in the center. Flatten it slightly with a rolling pin to a thickness of ⅛ "to form a rectangle of 18 x 12 inches, and sprinkle it liberally with sugar. Using a pastry cutter, cut the dough into ¾ x 2 inch strips. Lift each strip; twist it in the center to create a bow. Line a cookie sheet with parchment paper and place the bows ½ inch apart. Bake at 400°F for the first few minutes until they turn on their sides. Lower the heat to 200°F and continue baking 25-30 minutes on the middle rack of the oven, until cookies are hard to the touch at all corners and look golden brown.

Test for doneness by breaking one bow in half. If it is too soft, it is not done yet. Return to oven for a few more minutes. Make sure the bows are completely dry. Cool and keep in an airtight container.

SUGAR COOKIES (Luba Hochner)

Serves 20

2	cups all-purpose flour
2	eggs
2	egg yolks
5	ounces unsalted butter
1	dash salt
¾	cup sugar

In an electric mixer, cream sugar, salt, and butter until a whitish color is acquired. Add eggs, one by one; add yolks. Gradually add flour and refrigerate the dough for one hour.

With wet or oiled hands, form small rolls. Dip one side in sugar and arrange it on a previously greased baking sheet, sugar side up and one inch apart. Bake in a preheated oven at 325°F for about 20 minutes. The cookies should still be white and not at all colored. They will be very soft and friable and seem uncooked, but will firm up as they cool. Remove from the paper only when they have hardened.

Cooking Tip:
Replace a ¼ cup of flour with ground almonds.

VANILLE KIPFERL

Serves 30–35

½	cup almonds, hazelnuts, or walnuts
2	cups all-purpose flour
7	ounces unsalted butter
3	tablespoons sugar
1	teaspoon vanilla extract or 2 packets vanilla sugar
¼	cup powdered sugar
1	dash salt

For coating the crescents:

½	cup powdered sugar

Finely grind the nuts. Sift the flour on the worktop and cut in the chilled butter. Add the almonds and sugar. Knead into a smooth pastry. Refrigerate for 1 hour. Pinch off walnut-sized pieces. With the palms of your hands, form a cylindrical rope with tapered ends; curve them gently into a half-moon shape. Put the crescents on a greased and floured cookie sheet; bake them at 300°F for about 18-20 minutes, or until they are slightly colored at the edges. (Crescents have to be pale gold.)

Prepare a large sheet of waxed paper and dredge generously with vanilla powdered sugar.

Remove the crescents from the oven and let them cool for two minutes. While still warm, lift the pastries one at the time between two forks, and roll them in the sugar until they are completely coated. Leave them to cool on a clean sheet of waxed paper on a wire rack. The cookies will keep fresh for several weeks if they are stored in an airtight container.

Cooking Tips:

Chill the butter.

To make vanilla flavored confectioners' sugar, fill a jar with the sugar and insert a piece of sliced-open vanilla bean. Cover the jar, shake it a few times, and store. It will take a few days to absorb the vanilla flavor.

If almonds are used, they have to be blanched and slightly toasted. Hazelnuts need to be toasted and peeled.

WAFER RHOMBOIDS (Dora Fleminger)

Serves 30

¾	cup honey
½	cup sugar
4	ounces unsalted butter
2	tablespoons fine crumbs (from ladyfingers)
6	ounces semi-sweet chocolate
1	cup walnuts
3	sheets torte wafers

Use three thin square torte wafers. In a small pot, mix all of the ingredients, except for the nuts, and bring them to a boil. Make crumbs from ladyfingers, or any other fine, plain cookies. Lower the heat and mix constantly for about three minutes. Coarsely chop the walnuts. Take out a few tablespoons of the chocolate mixture for frosting, before incorporating the nuts. Spread the filling between the three wafers and put something heavy on top and refrigerate until the next day. Refrigerate the frosting as well. Before spreading the frosting on the top wafer, let it reach room temperature. Remove the weight and decorate. Cut into 1½ inch strips and then cut them into squares or rhomboids.

WALNUT COOKIES

Serves 20

For the dough

2	eggs
1½	cups all-purpose flour
2	teaspoons lemon zest
1	teaspoons vanilla extract
¼	teaspoon baking powder
1¼	cups sugar
10	tablespoons unsalted butter
2	egg yolks

For the top

½	cup walnuts
¼	cup sugar
24	maraschino cherries
2	egg whites

Preheat the oven to 350°F. Line a cookie sheet with parchment paper. Sift the flour and baking powder. In an electric mixer, combine the butter, egg yolks (save the egg whites for the topping), lemon zest, vanilla, and the flour with the baking powder. Form about twenty to twenty-four balls

In a deep bowl, beat the egg whites with a fork. In a flat plate, mix the finely ground walnuts with the sugar. Dip each ball first in the egg white and then in the sugar/nuts mixture, being careful not to dip the bottom of the balls. Place the dipped balls on a flat cookie sheet, one inch apart. With the index fingertip, press the center of each ball and fill it with a maraschino cherry, or any red jam. Bake them for forty minutes, or until they are golden brown. Cool and lift them carefully from the parchment paper. Placing the cookies in a tightly closed box will keep them fresh for several weeks.

WEISSE BUSSERL (White biscuits)

Serves 18

For the dough

2½	cups all-purpose flour
3	egg yolks
2	tablespoons sugar
8	ounces unsalted butter

For the top

2	egg whites
¾	cup sugar

For the filling

1	cup raspberry or red currant jam

Mix together the butter, yolks, sugar, and flour. Roll out the dough on a floured surface and cut out round, thin cookies of 1½ inches in diameter. Place on a cookie sheet lined with parchment paper.

Beat the egg whites with the sugar to a meringue consistency. With a teaspoon, spread a little amount of meringue to cover each cookie. Bake at 350°F to a light color. Remove the cookies from the oven and let them cool. Carefully lift each cookie, spread a little bit of jam at the bottom, and put two together. They will look like small, white balls.

MISCELLANEOUS

BASIC BUTTER DOUGH

2½   cups all-purpose flour
1   cup unsalted butter
1   cup heavy whipping cream
1   dash salt
1   tablespoon sugar

Mix all of the ingredients and refrigerate the dough for one hour before use. This is good for any filling or form of small pastries like crescents or rugelach.

CURUBA FLUFF (Colombian specialty)

Serves 6

1	cup curuba juice
1	cup sugar
2½	tablespoons unflavored gelatin
¼	cup cold water
8	egg whites

Cook the juice with sugar until it comes to a boil. Remove it from the heat. Dissolve the gelatin in the cold water and add to the juice. Place the mixture in the refrigerator until it begins to grow firm. Remove it from the refrigerator, and beat it until it becomes foamy. Add stiffly beaten egg whites and serve in champagne glasses.

Cooking Tip:
The curuba fruit has a very distinct flavor, but any tropic fruit juice can be used instead.

DOUGH FOR STRUDEL (Lucie Sadmon)

Serves 14

For the dough

2	cups all-purpose flour
1	teaspoon baking powder
8	tablespoons unsalted butter or margarine
1	egg
3	teaspoons sour cream
1	egg yolk for the glaze

Sift the flour with the baking powder. In electric mixer knead all the ingredients to a soft but not sticky dough and refrigerate overnight. The next day, cut the dough into four equal parts. Roll out each part to about ¼ inch thick. Spread any filling ingredients on top and roll it up like a strudel. Close the ends and brush the dough with an egg yolk. Repeat procedure with all 4 parts. Bake at 350°F until the top is light brown.

Cooking Tip:
This dough can be filled with any sweet our salty mixtures.

POVIDLA (Lekvar/plum butter)

1	pound dried, pitted prunes
1	pound sugar
6	oranges
2	bay leaves
2	tablespoons honey

Put the prunes in a large pot and cover them with water. Cook them on low heat until they are tender. When the prunes are cool, puree them in a food processor or blender. Return them to the pot; add the juice of the oranges, the sugar, and the bay leaves. Cook stirring constantly until the mixture gets thick. Cool it and fill several jars with the prune jam. This can be kept refrigerated for many months.

SPICES

Use of spices:

For lamb: rosemary, bay leaf, and garlic

For pork: sage, rosemary, and garlic

For chicken: tarragon

For fish: chives

For salmon: fennel

For salads: basil and tarragon

STREUSEL TOPPING

1 cup coarsely chopped walnuts

1 cup sugar (can be brown)

½ cup all-purpose flour

½ stick unsalted butter or margarine

Mix all ingredients with a fork or by hand and sprinkle on top of any recipe that calls for a streusel topping.

PICKLED CUCUMBERS

2	pounds pickling Kirby or any skinny small cucumbers
6	cups water
3	tablespoons kosher salt if available
1	large bunch of fresh dill
8	unpeeled, smashed garlic cloves
1	teaspoon black peppercorns
2	bay leaves
1	slice dark bread

Rinse the cucumbers and pierce them in the center with a small, very sharp knife. Rinse the dill under running water, and cut off the roots. Place the cucumbers in a large glass jar with the garlic, peppercorns, and bay leaf.

Bring the water and salt to a boil, and pour it immediately over the cucumbers. Place the dill and bread slice on top. Make sure the cucumbers are entirely covered with water. Cover the jar with the lid, and place it in the warmest corner of the kitchen. Put a plate under the jar to prevent the fermenting liquid from spilling. The pickles should be ready in about six to eight days.

Discard the dill and the bread, and refrigerate. The pickles will keep fresh for several weeks.

᠁ TIPS ᠁

SUBSTITUTES

Self-rising flour: 1 cup = 1 cup all-purpose flour + 1¼ baking powder + ⅛ teaspoon salt

Sour cream: 1 cup = 7/8 cup buttermilk or yogurt + 3 tablespoons butter

Fresh yeast: 1 tablespoon = 1 packet of dry yeast

BREAD SPICES

1	teaspoon ground or whole caraway seeds
1	teaspoon ground coriander seeds
1	teaspoon ground fennel seeds

When baking any multigrain or dark bread, add these spices.

Peeling skins of roasted bell peppers: Place the peppers in a pan with a tight fitting lid or in a strong brown paper bag and twist it closed.

Cooking cabbage or cauliflower: Add a little vinegar to the cooking water to reduce the odor.

Too much salt: Cut up a potato and boil it in the soup or stew. That will absorb the excess salt. Remove it before serving.

Meringues: Keep the eggs at room temperature to create a larger volume when whipping the egg whites.

Baking a cake or a pie with a meringue topping: As soon as the meringue is brown, turn off the oven, but leave the door ajar until the pie cools down to prevent it from splitting.

Keeping parchment paper in place: To prevent the parchment paper from curling up on the baking sheet, place one refrigerator magnet over each corner. Remove them before placing the cookies in the oven.

Lemon juice and zest: Buy a large bag of lemons and keep three to four in the refrigerator for near-future use. Before zesting, scrub the fruit with a sponge and warm, soapy water. Rinse it well and dry it with a paper towel. With a fine lemon grater scrape the yellow part of the peel and freeze in a small sandwich bag. Cut up the peeled lemons, squeeze out the juice, pour it into an ice cube tray, and freeze. Once frozen, transfer the cubes into a plastic bag, and keep them in the freezer.

ABOUT THE AUTHOR

Ruth Glasberg Gold was born in Bukovina, Romania (now Ukraine) and deported at eleven to a concentration camp in Transnistria, where her parents and only brother perished.

After the war she joined a Zionist youth commune, and escaped from communist Romania on a freighter, shipwrecked off a Greek Island. Rescued by the British, she was taken to a detention camp on the island of Cyprus. A year later she was freed to go to Palestine.

Together with her commune, she helped create a new kibbutz in the Judean Hills near Jerusalem, and later entered Hadassah Nursing School in Jerusalem graduating as an R.N.

In 1954 Ruth became head-nurse at Elisha Hospital, then supervisor at Rambam Hospital, both in Haifa.

In 1958 she married and left Israel for Bogota, Colombia, where her son and her daughter were born. In 1972 the family emigrated to Miami, Florida. She was widowed in 1982.

Ruth was a participant in *The International Study of Organized Persecution of Children*; co-founder of WIZO (Women's International Organization) in the U.S.A., founder of the first support group for child survivors of the Holocaust in Florida, and is a frequent speaker on the Holocaust. She is also a freelance interpreter in seven languages.

Ruth's Journey: A Survivor's Memoir University Press of Florida 1996, is her first book.

In February 2000 it has been translated into Hebrew and published in Israel by Yad Vashem, The Holocaust Martyr's and

Heroes" Remembrance Authority. In October 2003 the same book has been published in Romania by "Editura Hasefer" and in June 2008 in Spanish by "Editorial Font" in Mexico. The German translation has been published in 2009 by Edition Steinbauer GmbH in Vienna, Austria.

On January 27, 2009 Ruth was a guest speaker at the U.N. in N.Y., at the International Day of Commemoration of the Holocaust.

INDEX